AF717994

the Accepted Whispers

"Munājāt-e-Maqbūl"

the Accepted Whispers

"Munājāt-e-Maqbūl"

ٱدْعُوا۟ رَبَّكُمْ تَضَرُّعًا وَخُفْيَةً

Call on your Lord humbly and secretly...
(Al-Aʿrāf, 7:55)

مناجات مقبول

Compiled by
Mawlānā Ashraf ʿAlī Thānawī

Translation by
Khalid Baig

OVER 200 DUʿĀ'S FROM THE QUR'ĀN
AND ḤADĪTH FOR DAILY READING

openmind press
Garden Grove • California

Copyright © 2005, 2018 Khalid Baig.
All rights reserved. Aside from fair use, meaning a few pages or less for educational purposes, review, or scholarly citation, no part of this publication may be reproduced, stored in a retrieval system or transmitted in any form or by any means electronic, mechanical, photocopying, recording or otherwise, without the prior written permission of the copyright holder.

ISBN 978-0-9755157-5-4 (FLEXICOVER)
ISBN 978-0-9755157-3-0 (PAPERBACK)

Library of Congress Control Number: 2012919707

Pocket Size Edition Dhul Ḥijjah 1433 / November 2012
Flexicover Edition Dhul Ḥijjah 1439 / August 2018

PUBLISHED BY
Open Mind Press
PO Box 1338, Garden Grove, CA 92842
www.openmindpress.com

Typeset by Muneeb Baig
Cover image of Hassan II Mosque, Morocco by S. Desmond/Paintdrying.com

Printed and bound by Mega Printers, Turkey

This book is printed on acid-free paper.

To

محمد صلى الله عليه وسلم

Muḥammad, son of ʿAbdullāh
The Seal of the prophets,
The Mercy to the worlds.
His prayers are another gift of
mercy and compassion to us.
What would be life without them!
What would be life without him!

May Allah سبحانه وتعالى *shower His Blessings*
and Peace upon him,
his family, his Companions, and his followers

صلى الله عليه وسلم

Transliteration Key

ء (إ أ) (ئ)	' (a slight catch in the breath)
ا	a
ب	b
ت , ة	t (ة has an "h" sound at the end of a sentence)
ث	th (as in "thorn")
ج	j
ح	ḥ (heavy h)
خ	kh ("ch" in Scottish loch)
د	d (the hard "th" in "the")
ذ	dh (the soft "th" in "these")
ر	r
ز	z
س	s
ش	sh
ص	ṣ (heavy s, from the upper mouth)
ض	ḍ (heavy d, from the upper mouth)
ط	ṭ (heavy t, from the upper mouth)
ظ	ẓ (heavy z, from the upper mouth)
ع	' (like two a's from deep within the throat)
غ	gh (similar to French r)
ف	f
ق	q (heavy k, from the throat)
ك	k
ل	l
م	m
ن	n
ه	h (as in "help")
و	w
ي	y (as in "yellow")

Vowels

ـَ ـً	a (slightly softer than the "u" in "but"); an
ـِ ـٍ	i (as in "in"); in
ـُ ـٌ	u ("oo" in "book"); un
آ ا '	ā (elongated a, as when you would stretch the "a" in "plastic")
أ	ā at the start of a word, 'ā in the middle (pronounced like اَءَ)
و and ُ	ū ("u" in "glue")
ي and ِ	ī ("ee" in "feet")
ّ	stress symbol, indicated by repetition of letter

Honorifics

سبحانه وتعالى	Glorified and Most High	صلى الله عليه وسلم	Allah's blessings and peace be upon him
عليه السلام	May peace be upon him	رضي الله عنه , رضي الله عنها	May Allah be pleased with him/her

Contents

بِسْمِ اللَّهِ الرَّحْمَنِ الرَّحِيمِ

Introduction

Once Prophet Muḥammad ﷺ passed by a people who were suffering from some affliction. "Why don't they make *duʿā'* (supplication) to Allah for protection," he said. With all the suffering and disasters Muslims are facing in various parts of the world, the question can be directed to all of us today.

It is not that we have forgotten duʿā' completely; we refer to it regularly. But our ideas and practice regarding duʿā' have become distorted. Often it is reduced to the level of a ritual. Generally it is considered when all our efforts have failed—an act of last resort. It is belittled through actions and sometimes even with words. Is it any wonder that today mostly a mention of du'ā' is meant to indicate the hopelessness of a situation.

What a tragedy, for du'ā' is the most potent weapon of a believer. It can change fate, while no action of ours ever can. It is the essence of *'ibādah* (worship). With it we can never fail; without it we can never succeed. In the proper scheme of things, du'ā' should be the first and the last resort of the believer, with all his plans and actions coming in between. In every difficulty we ask Allah ﷿ to show us the way to handle that difficulty; we seek His help in following the path He shows to us; we seek His aid in making our efforts successful. When we fall sick, we know that we cannot find the right doctor without His Will; that the best doctor may not be able to diagnose our condition without His Command; that the best treatment plan will not succeed without His Permission. We make du'ā' for all of these. We make du'ā' before we seek medical help, while we are receiving it and after it has been delivered. The same is true of all other difficulties we may encounter.

Du'ā' is conversation with Allah ﷿, our Creator, our Lord and Master, the All Knowing, the

All Powerful. This act in itself is of extraordinary significance. It is the most uplifting, liberating, empowering, and transforming conversation a person can ever have. We turn to Him because we know that He alone can lift our sufferings and solve our problems. We feel relieved after describing our difficulties to our Creator. We feel empowered after having communicated with the All Mighty. We sense His mercy all around us after talking to the Most Merciful.

Allah ﷻ gave us life and everything that we possess, without our having any right to it. It is His design and it is with a purpose. Our conditions of health and sickness, our affluence and poverty, our joys and sorrows, our apparent successes and failures, our gains and losses—all of them are just a test. He "created death and life that He may test you which of you is best in deed" (*Al-Mulk*, 67:2).

Our ultimate success or failure—in the Hereafter—will depend solely on how we acted in the different circumstances that He chose for us. Did we seek His help when we needed help or were we too arrogant to ask? Did we accept His Will when things did not turn out our way? Did we show gratitude for His favors or were we proud of our own achievements?

We pray to Him because only He can give. He is not answerable to any authority and everyone is answerable to Him. He has power over everything and none can overpower Him. His knowledge is infinite while ours is infinitesimal compared to His. He is the Lord; we are His slaves. He may grant our duʿā's here; or He may reward us for them in the Hereafter; or He may give us something better than what we asked for.

We should make duʿā' for all things big and small. It is the beginning of wisdom to realize that "big" and "small" are arbitrary labels that are totally irrelevant in this context. Nothing is too big for the One we are asking from; nothing is too small for the one who is asking. That is why we have been taught to ask Allah ﷻ even when we need something as small as shoelaces. We should ask as a beggar, as a destitute person, for that is what we in reality are in relationship to Allah ﷻ. At the same time we should ask with great hope and conviction that we shall be granted our duʿā's, for a duʿā' lacking concentration and conviction is no duʿā' at all.

A praying person can never lose, for duʿāʾ is the highest form of submission to Him. "Prophet Muḥammad ﷺ was the best of mankind because he was the best in submission to Allah," says Mawlānā Manẓūr Nuʿmānī. "Anyone who studies his supplications cannot but be awestruck by the perfect understanding of our relationship to the Creator reflected by them." For this ummah, his duʿā's are one of his greatest spiritual gifts.

Quite naturally many scholars have collected them into separate books. Among these was *Al-Ḥiṣn al-Ḥaṣīn* (The Impregnable Fortress) by Muḥammad ibn Muḥammad al-Jazarī (751–833 AH), a well-known authority on Qurʾānic recitation, Ḥadīth, and Fiqh. The book was written in Dhul-Ḥijjah 791 AH when an invading army had sieged Damascus. After a few days of reciting these duʿā's by the compiler, the army suddenly left the helpless and frightened city. The event gave the book its popularity as a collection of duʿā's to be read for protection against calamities. It was divided into seven parts, one for each day of the week, to facilitate that reading.

Subsequently, *Al-Ḥizb al-Aʿẓam* (The Great Prayer Book) was organized for a daily reading by its compiler Mullā ʿAlī al-Qārī (d. 1014 AH). This has the advantage that these duʿā's can become a part of our daily schedule. One may find that the best part of his day is the one dedicated to these duʿā's. Additionally after some time one may find that he has memorized a large number of these duʿā's without any special effort. He may then find himself saying these duʿā's at other occasions also, for which they are particularly suited.

The Accepted Whispers is a translation of *Munājāt-e-Maqbūl*, which was patterned after and drew from *Al-Ḥizb*. It was compiled by Mawlānā Ashraf ʿAlī Thānawī as *Qurubāt ʿIndAllāhi wa Ṣalawāt ar-Rasūl* (Prayers that Bring One Close to Allah and the Invocations of the Messenger) and translated into Urdu poetry and prose by his associates. The translation was given the title "Munājāt-e-Maqbūl." Like his *Bihishtī Zewar* (Heavenly Ornaments), *Munājāt-e-Maqbūl* has been very popular in the countries of the Indian subcontinent, where it has become a household name.

This pocket size edition is for people on the go. To keep the weight and costs down it only contains the Arabic text with brief references and English translation on the facing page. The larger edition, published since 2005, provides transliteration, commentary, and detailed references in Arabic as well. The commentary aims at providing explanation as well as special merits or historic background of the duʿā'. This should help enhance our understanding of the meaning and significance of the duʿā's thereby helping us derive much greater benefit from them. Readers might like to keep the full edition at home.

In preparing this book, the Arabic text of published editions of *Munājāt* was compared with the books of Ḥadīth and changes were made wherever deemed necessary. Also, existing editions of *Munājāt* contained many typographical errors. These have been fixed. The pocket size edition was prepared from the fourth printing of the larger book.

We need duʿā's in all circumstances and all times. But in the dark ages that we are living in today, we need them even more. Every day brings fresh news about atrocities committed against our brothers and sisters around the world. What can we do? We can continue to just feel frustrated and depressed. We can just forget all this and move on to some other subject. Or we can stand up before Allah سبحانه وتعالى and pray for His help, Who alone can help. The duʿā' can change our life, our outlook, and our fate. It is the most potent weapon of a believer. May Allah سبحانه وتعالى make this book an instrument of delivering that power to us.

I request the readers to kindly remember me, my family, and everyone who helped in the publication of this book in their duʿā's.

Khalid Baig

20 Dhul Qaʿdah 1433 / 6 October 2012

Prayer (دعاء) and its Etiquettes

THE QUR'ĀN AND ḤADĪTH LITERATURE tell us about the extraordinary importance of praying to Allah ﷻ for all our needs. They also teach us its proper etiquettes. This is a brief selection.

Significance

وَقَالَ رَبُّكُمُ ٱدْعُونِيٓ أَسْتَجِبْ لَكُمْۚ إِنَّ ٱلَّذِينَ يَسْتَكْبِرُونَ عَنْ عِبَادَتِي سَيَدْخُلُونَ جَهَنَّمَ دَاخِرِينَ ﴿٦٠﴾

And your Lord says: Call on Me; I will answer your (Prayer): but those who are too arrogant to serve Me shall soon enter Hell—in humiliation. (*al-Ghāfir*, 40:60)

This verse uses the words duʿā' and ʿibādah interchangeably, thereby affirming that duʿā' is an act of worship.

وَإِذَا سَأَلَكَ عِبَادِى عَنِّى فَإِنِّى قَرِيبٌ ۖ أُجِيبُ دَعْوَةَ ٱلدَّاعِ إِذَا دَعَانِ ۖ فَلْيَسْتَجِيبُوا۟ لِى وَلْيُؤْمِنُوا۟ بِى لَعَلَّهُمْ يَرْشُدُونَ ﴿١٨٦﴾

And when My servants ask you concerning Me, surely I am very near; I answer the call of the caller when he calls on Me, so they should answer My call and believe in Me in order that they may be led aright. (*al-Baqarah*, 2:186)

مَنْ فُتِحَ لَهُ مِنْكُمْ بَابُ الدُّعَاءِ فُتِحَتْ لَهُ أَبْوَابُ الرَّحْمَةِ وَمَا سُئِلَ اللهُ شَيْئًا يَعْنِي أَحَبَّ إِلَيْهِ مِنْ أَنْ يُسْأَلَ الْعَافِيَةَ

Anyone of you for whom the door to duʿā' has been opened, the doors to mercy have been opened for him. And the thing that Allah likes most to be asked for is *ʿāfiyah* (health, security, protection). (*Sunan at-Tirmidhī* and *Ibn Mājah*)

مَنْ لَّمْ يَسْأَلِ اللهَ يَغْضَبْ عَلَيْهِ

Allah is angry with those who do not make supplications to Him. (*Sunan at-Tirmidhī*)

إِنَّ الْدُّعَاءَ يَنْفَعُ مِمَّا نَزَلَ وَمِمَّا لَمْ يَنْزِلْ، فَعَلَيْكُمْ عِبَادَ اللهِ بِالدُّعَاءِ

Du'ā' is beneficial regarding calamities that have fallen and calamities that have not fallen. So, servants of Allah, devote yourselves to du'ā'. (*Sunan at-Tirmidhī* and *Musnad Aḥmad*)

It means that du'ā' can prevent a disaster that was going to happen as well as lift the one that has already happened.

Attitude

ٱدْعُوا۟ رَبَّكُمْ تَضَرُّعًا وَخُفْيَةً ۚ إِنَّهُۥ لَا يُحِبُّ ٱلْمُعْتَدِينَ ﴿٥٥﴾

Call on your Lord humbly and secretly; surely He does not love those who exceed the limits. (*Al-A'rāf*, 7:55)

أُدْعُوْا اللهَ وَأَنْتُمْ مُّوْقِنُوْنَ بِالْإِجَابَةِ وَاعْلَمُوْا أَنَّ اللهَ لَا يَسْتَجِيْبُ دُعَاءً مِّنْ قَلْبٍ غَافِلٍ لَّاهٍ

Pray to Allah with the conviction that you will be answered and know that Allah does not answer a supplication that comes from a careless and inattentive heart. (*Sunan at-Tirmidhī*)

مَنْ سَرَّهُ أَنْ يَّسْتَجِيْبَ اللهُ لَهُ عِنْدَ الشَّدَائِدِ وَالْكُرَبِ فَلْيُكْثِرِ الدُّعَاءَ فِي الرَّخَاءِ

Whoever likes that Allah answer his duʿā's in hard times and periods of worry, he should abundantly make duʿā's in good times. (*Sunan at-Tirmidhī*)

Practice

1. Ḥalāl earnings and consumption are necessary for duʿā's to be answered

2. Pray for yourself before praying for others

There is great wisdom in this Prophetic teaching. We are all in need of Allah's mercy all the time. This practice will, inshā Allah, ensure that our duʿā's to

Allah for others do not lead us to think that we are superior to them.

3. BEGIN WITH ḤAMD AND ṢALĀT ʿALAN NABĪ AND END WITH ĀMĪN

There is consensus of ʿulamāʾ that *ḥamd* and *ṣalāt ʿalan Nabī* should be said in the beginning and end of every duʿāʾ session, whether in the ṣalāh or outside it.

4. REQUEST OTHERS TO PRAY FOR YOU

عَنْ عُمَرَ بْنِ الْخَطَّابِ قَالَ اسْتَأْذَنْتُ النَّبِيَّ صَلَّى اللهُ عَلَيْهِ وَسَلَّمَ فِي الْعُمْرَةِ فَأَذِنَ وَقَالَ أَشْرِكْنَا يَا أُخَيَّ فِي دُعَائِكَ وَلَا تَنْسَنَا فَقَالَ كَلِمَةً مَّا يَسُرُّنِيْ أَنَّ لِيْ بِهَا الدُّنْيَا (رواه أبو داود والترمذي)

ʿUmar ibn al-Khaṭṭāb ﵁ narrates: "I asked the Prophet ﷺ for permission to perform an ʿUmrah and he gave me permission saying, 'Dear brother, include us in your supplication and do not forget us.' This expression ('dear brother') that he said, I would not be willing to exchange it for the world." (*Sunan Abī Dāwūd* and *Sunan at-Tirmidhī*)

This ḥadīth shows that we should request those visiting the holy places to make duʿā' for us. It also shows that we can request our juniors for duʿā's.

Most Likely Accepted Duʿā's

ثَلٰثُ دَعَوَاتٍ مُّسْتَجَابَاتٌ لَّا شَكَّ فِيْهِنَّ: دَعْوَةُ الْوَالِدِ وَدَعْوَةُ الْمُسَافِرِ وَدَعْوَةُ الْمَظْلُومِ (رواه الترمذي وأبو داود وابن ماجه)

Three duʿā's are answered, there is no doubt about them: the duʿā' of a parent, the duʿā' of a traveler, and the duʿā' of the one who has been wronged. (*Sunan at-Tirmidhī*, *Sunan Abī Dāwūd*, and *Ibn Mājah*)

This has several implications. We should pray for our children. If we are fortunate that our parents are alive, we should request them for duʿā's and try to earn it by winning their hearts through our good treatment. We should take care of travelers (traveling for a good cause) so we can earn their duʿā's. And we must be very alert never to wrong any person, for Allah ﷻ accepts the duʿā' of the wronged. On the other hand we should help a person who has been wronged so he or she prays for us.

عَنْ أَبِيْ سَعِيْدٍ الْخُدْرِيِّ أَنَّ النَّبِيَّ صَلَّى اللهُ عَلَيْهِ وَسَلَّمَ قَالَ مَا مِنْ مُسْلِمٍ يَّدْعُو بِدَعْوَةٍ لَّيْسَ فِيْهَا إِثْمٌ وَلَا قَطِيْعَةُ رَحْمٍ إِلَّا أَعْطَاهُ اللهُ بِهَا إِحْدٰى ثَلٰثٍ إِمَّا أَنْ يُّعَجِّلَ لَهُ دَعْوَتَهُ وَإِمَّا أَنْ يَّدَّخِرَهَا لَهُ فِي الْاٰخِرَةِ وَإِمَّا أَنْ يَّصْرِفَ عَنْهُ مِنَ السُّوْءِ مِثْلَهَا قَالُوْا إِذًا نُّكْثِرُ قَالَ اللهُ أَكْثَرُ (رواه أحمد)

Abū Saʿīd al-Khudrī ﵁ narrates that the Prophet ﷺ said: "There is no Muslim who makes a duʿā', as long as the duʿā' contains nothing that is sinful or involves breaking family ties, except that Allah will give him one of three things: He will grant him in this world what he asked for, or save the reward for him for the Hereafter, or turn away from him a similar hardship (that would have afflicted him in the absence of that duʿā')." The Companions said, "Then we will greatly increase (our duʿā's)." He replied, "Allah has even more." (*Musnad Aḥmad*)

About Mawlānā Ashraf ʿAlī Thānawī

Mawlānā Ashraf ʿAlī Thānawī, (1280-1362 AH / 1863-1943 CE), commonly referred to as *Ḥakīm al-Ummat* ("Sage of the Ummah"), was a giant among the Islamic scholars of the twentieth century. He was a master in all branches of Islamic scholarship including Qur'ān, Ḥadīth, Fiqh and Taṣawwuf. A prolific writer, he had more than a thousand publications to his credit. He wrote for the minimally literate as effectively as he did for scholars. Nearly a century later some of his books remain as popular as they were when originally published. Mufti Muhammad Taqi Usmani writes, "The likeness of his accomplishments is not found in many preceding centuries."

A Duʿāʾ

composed by Mawlānā Ashraf ʿAlī Thānawī

نَحْمَدُكَ يَا خَيْرَ مَأْمُولٍ، وَأَكْرَمَ مَسْئُوْلٍ، عَلٰى مَا
عَلَّمْتَنَا مِنَ الْمُنَاجَاتِ المَقْبُولِ، مِنْ قُرُبَاتٍ عِنْدَ اللهِ
وَ صَلَوَاتِ الرَّسُوْلِ. فَصَلِّ عَلَيْهِ مَا اخْتَلَفَ الدَّبُوْرُ
وَالْقَبُوْلُ، وَانْشَعَبَتِ الْفُرُوْعُ مِنَ الْأُصُوْلِ. ثُمَّ
نَسْأَلُكَ بِمَا سَنَقُوْلُ. وَمِنَّا السُّؤَالُ وَمِنْكَ الْقُبُوْلُ.

We praise You, O the Best of those in Whom hopes can be placed and the Most Generous of those who can be beseeched, for teaching us the Accepted Whispers. Taken from the book Qurubāt ʿIndAllāhi wa Ṣalawāt ar-Rasūl (Prayers that Bring One Close to Allah and the Invocations of the Messenger). Bless him (the Messenger ﷺ) as long as the westerly and easterly winds blow and branches continue to grow from the roots (i.e. until the Day of Judgment). We beg You in the words that follow (in the rest of the book). Asking is from us and acceptance is from you.

SATURDAY

In the Name of Allah, the Most Compassionate, the Most Merciful

(1) Our Lord, give us in this world that which is good and in the Hereafter that which is good, and protect us from the punishment of the Fire.

(2) Our Lord, pour out patience on us, plant firmly our feet, and give us victory over the disbelieving people.

(3) Our Lord, do not take us to task if we forget or make a mistake. Our Lord, do not place such a burden on us as You had placed on those before us. Our Lord, burden us not with that which we have not the strength to bear. Pardon us, grant us forgiveness, and have mercy on us. You are our Protector so help us to victory over the disbelieving people.

1 [*Al-Baqarah*, 2:201]

2 [*Al-Baqarah*, 2:250]

3 [*Al-Baqarah*, 2:286]

بِسْمِ اللَّهِ الرَّحْمَٰنِ الرَّحِيمِ

﴿١﴾ رَبَّنَآ ءَاتِنَا فِي الدُّنْيَا حَسَنَةً وَفِي الْآخِرَةِ حَسَنَةً
وَقِنَا عَذَابَ النَّارِ ۝

﴿٢﴾ رَبَّنَآ أَفْرِغْ عَلَيْنَا صَبْرًا وَثَبِّتْ أَقْدَامَنَا وَانْصُرْنَا
عَلَى الْقَوْمِ الْكَٰفِرِينَ ۝

﴿٣﴾ رَبَّنَا لَا تُؤَاخِذْنَآ إِنْ نَّسِينَآ أَوْ أَخْطَأْنَا ۚ رَبَّنَا
وَلَا تَحْمِلْ عَلَيْنَآ إِصْرًا كَمَا حَمَلْتَهُۥ عَلَى الَّذِينَ مِنْ
قَبْلِنَا ۚ رَبَّنَا وَلَا تُحَمِّلْنَا مَا لَا طَاقَةَ لَنَا بِهِۦ ۖ وَاعْفُ
عَنَّا وَاغْفِرْ لَنَا وَارْحَمْنَا ۚ أَنْتَ مَوْلَٰنَا فَانْصُرْنَا عَلَى
الْقَوْمِ الْكَٰفِرِينَ ۝

(4) Our Lord, do not let our hearts swerve after You have guided us, and grant us mercy from Your presence. Surely You are the most generous Grantor.

(5) Our Lord, surely we have believed, so forgive us our sins and shield us from the punishment of the Fire.

(6) Our Lord, You have not created all this in vain! Glory be to You; shield us then from the punishment of the Fire.

(7) Our Lord, surely whomsoever You sentence to the Fire, You have disgraced him indeed. And for wrongdoers there will be no supporters.

(8) Our Lord, surely we heard a caller calling to the faith, saying: believe in your Lord. And we believed. Our Lord, forgive us therefore our sins, and blot out from us our evil deeds, and in death join us

---

4 [*Āl-i-ʿImrān*, 3:8]

5 [*Āl-i-ʿImrān*, 3:16]

6 [*Āl-i-ʿImrān*, 3:191]

7 [*Āl-i-ʿImrān*, 3:192]

8 [*Āl-i-ʿImrān*, 3:193]

﴿٤﴾ رَبَّنَا لَا تُزِغْ قُلُوبَنَا بَعْدَ إِذْ هَدَيْتَنَا وَهَبْ لَنَا
مِن لَّدُنكَ رَحْمَةً ۚ إِنَّكَ أَنتَ الْوَهَّابُ ۝

﴿٥﴾ رَبَّنَآ إِنَّنَآ ءَامَنَّا فَاغْفِرْ لَنَا ذُنُوبَنَا وَقِنَا عَذَابَ
النَّارِ ۝

﴿٦﴾ رَبَّنَا مَا خَلَقْتَ هَٰذَا بَٰطِلًا سُبْحَٰنَكَ فَقِنَا
عَذَابَ النَّارِ ۝

﴿٧﴾ رَبَّنَآ إِنَّكَ مَن تُدْخِلِ النَّارَ فَقَدْ أَخْزَيْتَهُۥ ۖ وَمَا
لِلظَّٰلِمِينَ مِنْ أَنصَارٍ ۝

﴿٨﴾ رَبَّنَآ إِنَّنَا سَمِعْنَا مُنَادِيًا يُنَادِي لِلْإِيمَٰنِ أَنْ
ءَامِنُوا۟ بِرَبِّكُمْ فَـَٔامَنَّا ۚ رَبَّنَا فَاغْفِرْ لَنَا ذُنُوبَنَا وَكَفِّرْ عَنَّا
سَيِّـَٔاتِنَا وَتَوَفَّنَا مَعَ الْأَبْرَارِ ۝

with the righteous.

(9) *Our Lord, grant us what You have promised to us through Your messengers, and do not disgrace us on the Day of Judgment; surely You never break Your promise.*

(10) *Our Lord, we have wronged our souls. And if You do not forgive us and grant us mercy, we shall certainly be among the losers.*

(11) *Our Lord, pour out patience over us and make us die as Muslims.*

(12) *You are our Protector. So forgive us and show us mercy, for You are the best of those who forgive.*

(13) *Our Lord, do not make us an object of persecution for the oppressors and save us by Your mercy from the disbelieving people.*

---

9 [*Āl-i-ʿImrān*, 3:194]

10 [*Al-Aʿrāf*, 7:23]

11 [*Al-Aʿrāf*, 7:126]

12 [*Al-Aʿrāf*, 7:155]

13 [*Yūnus*, 10:85-86]

﴿٩﴾ رَبَّنَا وَاٰتِنَا مَا وَعَدْتَّنَا عَلٰى رُسُلِكَ وَلَا تُخْزِنَا
يَوْمَ الْقِيٰمَةِ ؕ إِنَّكَ لَا تُخْلِفُ الْمِيْعَادَ ۝

﴿١٠﴾ رَبَّنَا ظَلَمْنَآ أَنْفُسَنَا وَإِنْ لَّمْ تَغْفِرْ لَنَا وَتَرْحَمْنَا
لَنَكُوْنَنَّ مِنَ الْخٰسِرِيْنَ ۝

﴿١١﴾ رَبَّنَآ أَفْرِغْ عَلَيْنَا صَبْرًا وَّتَوَفَّنَا مُسْلِمِيْنَ ۝

﴿١٢﴾ أَنْتَ وَلِيُّنَا فَاغْفِرْ لَنَا وَارْحَمْنَا ۖ وَأَنْتَ خَيْرُ
الْغٰفِرِيْنَ ۝

﴿١٣﴾ رَبَّنَا لَا تَجْعَلْنَا فِتْنَةً لِّلْقَوْمِ الظّٰلِمِيْنَ ۝
وَنَجِّنَا بِرَحْمَتِكَ مِنَ الْقَوْمِ الْكٰفِرِيْنَ ۝

(14) O the Creator of the heavens and the earth, You are my Protector in this world and in the Hereafter. Make me die a Muslim and unite me with the righteous.

(15) My Lord, make me and my offspring establish ṣalāh. Our Lord, accept my supplication.

(16) Our Lord, forgive me and my parents and all believers on the day when the Reckoning will be set up.

(17) My Lord, show them (my parents) mercy just as they cared for me when I was a little child.

(18) My Lord, make me enter through a rightful entrance and leave by a rightful exit and grant me supporting authority from Your presence.

---

14 [*Yūsuf*, 12:101]

15 [*Ibrāhīm*, 14:40]

16 [*Ibrāhīm*, 14:41]

17 [*Al-Isrā'*, 17:24]

18 [*Al-Isrā'*, 17:80]

﴿١٤﴾ فَاطِرَ السَّمٰوٰتِ وَالْأَرْضِ أَنْتَ وَلِيّٖ
فِي الدُّنْيَا وَالْاٰخِرَةِ ۚ تَوَفَّنِيْ مُسْلِمًا وَّأَلْحِقْنِيْ
بِالصّٰلِحِيْنَ ۝

﴿١٥﴾ رَبِّ اجْعَلْنِيْ مُقِيْمَ الصَّلٰوةِ وَمِنْ ذُرِّيَّتِيْ ۚ
رَبَّنَا وَتَقَبَّلْ دُعَاءِ ۝

﴿١٦﴾ رَبَّنَا اغْفِرْ لِيْ وَلِوٰلِدَيَّ وَلِلْمُؤْمِنِيْنَ يَوْمَ
يَقُوْمُ الْحِسَابُ ۝

﴿١٧﴾ رَبِّ ارْحَمْهُمَا كَمَا رَبَّيٰنِيْ صَغِيْرًا ۝

﴿١٨﴾ رَبِّ أَدْخِلْنِيْ مُدْخَلَ صِدْقٍ وَّأَخْرِجْنِيْ
مُخْرَجَ صِدْقٍ وَّاجْعَلْ لِّيْ مِنْ لَّدُنْكَ سُلْطٰنًا
نَّصِيْرًا ۝

(19) Our Lord, grant us mercy from Your presence and provide us with guidance in our affair.

(20) My Lord, expand my breast for me, make my task easy for me, and untie a knot from my tongue so they may understand my speech.

(21) My Lord, increase me in knowledge.

(22) Adversity has afflicted me and You are the Most Merciful of the merciful.

(23) My Lord, leave me not childless, even though You are the Best of heirs.

(24) My Lord, make my landing a blessed landing, for You are the Best of those who bring (someone) to land.

---

19 [*Al-Kahf*, 18:10]

20 [*Ṭā-Hā*, 20:25-28]

21 [*Ṭā-Hā*, 20:114]

22 [*Al-Anbiyā'*, 21:83]

23 [*Al-Anbiyā'*, 21:89]

24 [*Al-Mu'minūn*, 23:29]

﴿١٩﴾ رَبَّنَآ اٰتِنَا مِنْ لَّدُنْكَ رَحْمَةً وَّهَيِّئْ لَنَا مِنْ
أَمْرِنَا رَشَدًا ۝

﴿٢٠﴾ رَبِّ اشْرَحْ لِيْ صَدْرِيْ ۝ وَيَسِّرْ لِيْ
أَمْرِيْ ۝ وَاحْلُلْ عُقْدَةً مِّنْ لِّسَانِيْ ۝ يَفْقَهُوْا
قَوْلِيْ ۝

﴿٢١﴾ رَبِّ زِدْنِيْ عِلْمًا ۝

﴿٢٢﴾ أَنِّيْ مَسَّنِيَ الضُّرُّ وَأَنْتَ أَرْحَمُ الرّٰحِمِيْنَ ۝

﴿٢٣﴾ رَبِّ لَا تَذَرْنِيْ فَرْدًا وَّأَنْتَ خَيْرُ
الْوَارِثِيْنَ ۝

﴿٢٤﴾ رَبِّ أَنْزِلْنِيْ مُنْزَلًا مُّبٰرَكًا وَّأَنْتَ خَيْرُ
الْمُنْزِلِيْنَ ۝

(25) *My Lord, I seek refuge with You from the promptings of the shayṭāns (devils) and I seek refuge with You, my Lord, even from their coming near me.*

(26) *Our Lord, we believe, so forgive us, and have mercy on us. You are the Best One to show mercy.*

(27) *Our Lord, turn away from us the punishment of Hell; surely its punishment is a persisting affliction.*

(28) *Our Lord, grant us the delight of our eyes in our spouses and our offspring and make us a model for the God-fearing.*

(29) *My Lord, enable me to be ever thankful for Your favor that You have bestowed on me and on my parents, and to do the good deeds that You are pleased with. And admit me through Your mercy among Your pious servants.*

---

25 [*Al-Mu'minūn*, 23:97-98]

26 [*Al-Mu'minūn*, 23:109]

27 [*Al-Furqān*, 25:65]

28 [*Al-Furqān*, 25:74]

29 [*An-Naml*, 27:19]

﴿٢٥﴾ رَبِّ أَعُوْذُ بِكَ مِنْ هَمَزٰتِ الشَّيٰطِيْنِ ۝
وَأَعُوْذُ بِكَ رَبِّ أَنْ يَّحْضُرُوْنِ ۝

﴿٢٦﴾ رَبَّنَآ اٰمَنَّا فَاغْفِرْ لَنَا وَارْحَمْنَا وَأَنْتَ خَيْرُ
الرّٰحِمِيْنَ ۝

﴿٢٧﴾ رَبَّنَا اصْرِفْ عَنَّا عَذَابَ جَهَنَّمَ صلے إِنَّ عَذَابَهَا
كَانَ غَرَامًا ۝

﴿٢٨﴾ رَبَّنَا هَبْ لَنَا مِنْ أَزْوَاجِنَا وَذُرِّيّٰتِنَا قُرَّةَ
أَعْيُنٍ وَّاجْعَلْنَا لِلْمُتَّقِيْنَ إِمَامًا ۝

﴿٢٩﴾ رَبِّ أَوْزِعْنِيْ أَنْ أَشْكُرَ نِعْمَتَكَ الَّتِيْ
أَنْعَمْتَ عَلَيَّ وَعَلٰى وَالِدَيَّ وَأَنْ أَعْمَلَ صَالِحًا تَرْضٰهُ
وَأَدْخِلْنِيْ بِرَحْمَتِكَ فِيْ عِبَادِكَ الصّٰلِحِيْنَ ۝

(30) *My Lord, I am needy of whatever good You send down for me.*

(31) *My Lord, help me against the mischievous people.*

(32) *Our Lord, Your mercy and knowledge encompass everything, therefore forgive those who repent and follow Your Way and shield them from the punishment of the Hell.*

(33) *Our Lord, admit them to the Gardens of Eternity that You have promised to them and to the righteous among their parents, spouses, and descendants. You are the Powerful, the Wise. And shield them from (all) ills; and any whom You do shield from ills that Day, on them surely You have bestowed mercy. And that is the supreme achievement, indeed.*

---

30 [*Al-Qaṣaṣ*, 28:24]

31 [*Al-ʿAnkabūt*, 29:30]

32 [*Ghāfir*, 40:7]

33 [*Ghāfir*, 40:8-9]

﴿٣٠﴾ رَبِّ إِنِّيْ لِمَآ أَنزَلْتَ إِلَيَّ مِنْ خَيْرٍ فَقِيْرٌ ۝

﴿٣١﴾ رَبِّ انْصُرْنِيْ عَلَى الْقَوْمِ الْمُفْسِدِيْنَ ۝

﴿٣٢﴾ رَبَّنَا وَسِعْتَ كُلَّ شَيْءٍ رَّحْمَةً وَّعِلْمًا فَاغْفِرْ
لِلَّذِيْنَ تَابُوْا وَاتَّبَعُوْا سَبِيْلَكَ وَقِهِمْ عَذَابَ
الْجَحِيْمِ ۝

﴿٣٣﴾ رَبَّنَا وَأَدْخِلْهُمْ جَنّٰتِ عَدْنِ الَّتِيْ وَعَدْتَّهُمْ
وَمَنْ صَلَحَ مِنْ اٰبَائِهِمْ وَأَزْوَاجِهِمْ وَذُرِّيّٰتِهِمْ ۚ إِنَّكَ
أَنْتَ الْعَزِيْزُ الْحَكِيْمُ ۝ وَقِهِمُ السَّيِّئَاتِ ۚ وَمَنْ
تَقِ السَّيِّئَاتِ يَوْمَئِذٍ فَقَدْ رَحِمْتَهُ ۚ وَذٰلِكَ هُوَ الْفَوْزُ
الْعَظِيْمُ ۝

(34) And grant for my benefit goodness in my progeny. Truly I have turned to You repentant and truly I am one of those who submit to You.

(35) I have been overpowered so help me.

(36) Our Lord, forgive us and those of our brethren who preceded us in faith, and do not allow any spite to remain in our hearts toward the believers. Our Lord, surely You are Full of Kindness, Most Merciful.

(37) Our Lord, in You we put our trust, and to You do we turn in repentance, and to You is the eventual destiny.

(38) Our Lord, do not subject us to persecution by the disbelievers, and forgive us, our Lord. Indeed You alone are the Exalted in Might, the Wise.

---

34 [*Al-Aḥqāf*, 46:15]

35 [*Al-Qamar*, 54:10]

36 [*Al-Ḥashr*, 59:10]

37 [*Al-Mumtaḥinah*, 60:4]

38 [*Al-Mumtaḥinah*, 60:5]

﴿٣٤﴾ وَأَصْلِحْ لِيْ فِيْ ذُرِّيَّتِيْ ۖ إِنِّيْ تُبْتُ إِلَيْكَ وَإِنِّيْ
مِنَ الْمُسْلِمِيْنَ ۝

﴿٣٥﴾ أَنِّيْ مَغْلُوْبٌ فَانْتَصِرْ ۝

﴿٣٦﴾ رَبَّنَا اغْفِرْ لَنَا وَلِإِخْوَانِنَا الَّذِيْنَ سَبَقُوْنَا
بِالْإِيْمَانِ وَلَا تَجْعَلْ فِيْ قُلُوْبِنَا غِلًّا لِّلَّذِيْنَ اٰمَنُوْا
رَبَّنَآ إِنَّكَ رَءُوْفٌ رَّحِيْمٌ ۝

﴿٣٧﴾ رَبَّنَا عَلَيْكَ تَوَكَّلْنَا وَإِلَيْكَ أَنَبْنَا وَإِلَيْكَ
الْمَصِيْرُ ۝

﴿٣٨﴾ رَبَّنَا لَا تَجْعَلْنَا فِتْنَةً لِّلَّذِيْنَ كَفَرُوْا وَاغْفِرْ لَنَا
رَبَّنَآ ۖ إِنَّكَ أَنْتَ الْعَزِيْزُ الْحَكِيْمُ ۝

(39) Our Lord, perfect our light for us, and forgive us. Surely You have power over all things.

(40) O my Lord, forgive me, my parents, all who enter my house in a state of belief, and (all) believing men and believing women.

(41) O Allah, wash away my sins with snow and hail water and purify my heart of sins as a white garment is cleansed of soil. And distance my sins as far away from me as You have distanced the east from the west.

(42) O Allah, bestow on my soul its taqwā. Purify it, for You are the Best of those who can purify it. You alone are its Guardian and Master.

(43) O Allah, we ask You for every good that Your prophet Muḥammad ﷺ asked You for.

---

39 [*At-Taḥrīm*, 66:8]

40 [*Nūḥ*, 71:28]

41 ['Ā'ishah. *Ṣaḥīḥ al-Bukhārī* #5898]

42 [Zayd ibn Arqam. *Ṣaḥīḥ Muslim* #4899]

43 [Abū Umāmah al-Bāhilī. *Sunan at-Tirmidhī* #3443]

﴿٣٩﴾ رَبَّنَآ أَتْمِمْ لَنَا نُوْرَنَا وَاغْفِرْ لَنَآ ۖ إِنَّكَ عَلىٰ كُلِّ
شَيْءٍ قَدِيْرٌ ۝

﴿٤٠﴾ رَبِّ اغْفِرْ لِيْ وَلِوَالِدَيَّ وَلِمَنْ دَخَلَ بَيْتِيَ
مُؤْمِنًا وَّلِلْمُؤْمِنِيْنَ وَالْمُؤْمِنَاتِ۔

﴿٤١﴾ اَللّٰهُمَّ اغْسِلْ خَطَايَايَ بِمَاءِ الثَّلْجِ وَالْبَرَدِ،
وَنَقِّ قَلْبِيْ مِنَ الْخَطَايَا كَمَا يُنَقَّى الثَّوْبُ الْأَبْيَضُ
مِنَ الدَّنَسِ، وَبَاعِدْ بَيْنِيْ وَبَيْنَ خَطَايَايَ كَمَا
بَاعَدْتَّ بَيْنَ الْمَشْرِقِ وَالْمَغْرِبِ۔

﴿٤٢﴾ اَللّٰهُمَّ اٰتِ نَفْسِيْ تَقْوَاهَا، وَزَكِّهَا أَنْتَ خَيْرُ
مَنْ زَكَّاهَا، أَنْتَ وَلِيُّهَا وَمَوْلَاهَا۔

﴿٤٣﴾ اَللّٰهُمَّ إِنَّا نَسْأَلُكَ مِنْ خَيْرِ مَا سَأَلَكَ مِنْهُ
نَبِيُّكَ مُحَمَّدٌ صَلَّى اللهُ عَلَيْهِ وَسَلَّمَ۔

(44) O Allah, we beg You for the means of Your forgiveness, for the deeds that will lead to salvation, for safety from all sins, for a share in every piety, for attainment of Paradise, and for freedom from Hell.

(45) O Allah, I beg You for beneficial knowledge.

(46) O Allah, forgive my sins, both unintentional and intentional.

(47) O Allah, forgive my errors, my ignorance, my excesses in my affairs, and those of my wrongs that you know better than I.

(48) O Allah, forgive my sins that I committed earnestly and those that I committed in jest.

(49) O Allah, the Turner of hearts, keep our hearts turned to your obedience.

---

44 [ʿAbdullāh ibn Masʿūd. *Mustadrak Ḥākim* #157/1957]

45 [Jābir ibn ʿAbdillāh. *Kanz al-ʿUmmāl* #3787]

46 [ʿUthmān ibn Abil-ʿĀṣ. *Musnad Aḥmad* #17229]

47 [Abū Mūsā al-Ashʿarī. *Ṣaḥīḥ al-Bukhārī* #5920]

48 [Abū Mūsā al-Ashʿarī. *Ṣaḥīḥ Muslim* #4896]

49 [ʿAbdullāh ibn ʿAmr ibn al-ʿĀṣ. *Ṣaḥīḥ Muslim* #4798]

﴿٤٤﴾ إِنَّا نَسْأَلُكَ عَزَائِمَ مَغْفِرَتِكَ، وَمُنْجِيَاتِ أَمْرِكَ، وَالسَّلَامَةَ مِنْ كُلِّ إِثْمٍ، وَّالغَنِيْمَةَ مِنْ كُلِّ بِرٍّ، وَّالْفَوْزَ بِالْجَنَّةِ، وَالنَّجَاةَ مِنَ النَّارِ۔

﴿٤٥﴾ اَللّٰهُمَّ إِنِّيْ أَسْأَلُكَ عِلْمًا نَّافِعًا۔

﴿٤٦﴾ اَللّٰهُمَّ اغْفِرْ لِيْ ذَنْبِيْ خَطَئِيْ وَعَمَدِيْ۔

﴿٤٧﴾ اَللّٰهُمَّ اغْفِرْ لِيْ خَطِيْئَتِيْ وَجَهْلِيْ، وَإِسْرَافِيْ فِيْ أَمْرِيْ، وَمَا أَنْتَ أَعْلَمُ بِهٖ مِنِّيْ۔

﴿٤٨﴾ اَللّٰهُمَّ اغْفِرْ لِيْ جِدِّيْ وَهَزْلِيْ۔

﴿٤٩﴾ اَللّٰهُمَّ مُصَرِّفَ الْقُلُوْبِ صَرِّفْ قُلُوْبَنَا عَلٰى طَاعَتِكَ۔

(50) O Allah, give me guidance and keep me firm (on the path of guidance).

(51) O Allah, I beg You for guidance, piety, chastity, and contentment.

(52) O Allah, put in order for me my religion, which is my protection. Put in order for me my material world in which lies my livelihood. Put in order for me my life to come to which is my return. Make life a means of increase for me in all that is good, and death a respite for me from every evil.

(53) O Allah, forgive my sins, have mercy on me, give me health and safety, and provide me with sustenance.

(54) O Allah, I seek Your protection from help-

50 [ʿAlī ibn Abī Ṭālib. *Ṣaḥīḥ Muslim* #4904]

51 [ʿAbdullāh ibn Masʿūd. *Ṣaḥīḥ Muslim* #4898]

52 [Abū Hurayrah. *Ṣaḥīḥ Muslim* #4897]

53 [Ṭāriq al-Ashjaʿī. *Ṣaḥīḥ Muslim* #4865]

54 [Composite: Anas ibn Mālik. *Mustadrak Ḥākim* #144/1944; ʿĀ'ishah. *Ṣaḥīḥ al-Bukhārī* #5898; Ibid. *Ṣaḥīḥ al-Bukhārī* #789; Anas ibn Mālik. *Ṣaḥīḥ al-Bukhārī* #2679; Saʿd ibn Abī Waqqāṣ. *Ṣaḥīḥ al-Bukhārī* #2610; Zayd ibn Arqam. *Ṣaḥīḥ Muslim* #4899]

﴿٥٠﴾ اَللّٰهُمَّ اهْدِنِيْ وَسَدِّدْنِيْ۔

﴿٥١﴾ اَللّٰهُمَّ إِنِّيْ أَسْأَلُكَ الْهُدٰى وَالتُّقٰى وَالْعَفَافَ وَالْغِنٰى۔

﴿٥٢﴾ اَللّٰهُمَّ أَصْلِحْ لِيْ دِيْنِيَ الَّذِيْ هُوَ عِصْمَةُ أَمْرِيْ، وَأَصْلِحْ لِيْ دُنْيَايَ الَّتِيْ فِيْهَا مَعَاشِيْ، وَأَصْلِحْ لِيْ اٰخِرَتِيَ الَّتِيْ فِيْهَا مَعَادِيْ، وَاجْعَلِ الْحَيٰوةَ زِيَادَةً لِّيْ فِيْ كُلِّ خَيْرٍ، وَّاجْعَلِ الْمَوْتَ رَاحَةً لِّيْ مِنْ كُلِّ شَرٍّ۔

﴿٥٣﴾ اَللّٰهُمَّ اغْفِرْ لِيْ وَارْحَمْنِيْ وَعَافِنِيْ وَارْزُقْنِيْ۔

﴿٥٤﴾ اَللّٰهُمَّ إِنِّيْ أَعُوْذُ بِكَ مِنَ الْعَجْزِ، وَالْكَسَلِ،

lessness, lethargy, cowardice, senility, burdensome liability, and sinfulness; from the punishment of Fire, the ordeal of Fire, the tribulation of the grave, the punishment in the grave, and the evil tribulations of affluence and of poverty; from the evil tribulation of the anointed Dajjāl (Antichrist); from the tests of life and death; from the hardness of heart, heedlessness, economic dependence, humiliation, indigence, unbelief, transgression, dissension, and seeking fame and showing off; from deafness, dumbness, lunacy, leprosy, and all painful diseases; from the burden of debt, worries, grief, stinginess, and coercion of the people; from reaching debilitating old age; and from the tribulations of this world, the knowledge that does not benefit, the heart that does not fear Allah, the soul that is never satiated, and the du'ā' that is not accepted.

وَالْجُبْنِ، وَالْهَرَمِ، وَالْمَغْرَمِ، وَالْمَأْثَمِ، وَمِنْ عَذَابِ
النَّارِ، وَفِتْنَةِ النَّارِ، وَفِتْنَةِ الْقَبْرِ، وَعَذَابِ الْقَبْرِ، وَشَرِّ
فِتْنَةِ الْغِنٰى، وَشَرِّ فِتْنَةِ الْفَقْرِ، وَمِنْ شَرِّ فِتْنَةِ الْمَسِيْحِ
الدَّجَّالِ، وَمِنْ فِتْنَةِ الْمَحْيَا وَالْمَمَاتِ، وَمِنَ الْقَسْوَةِ،
وَالْغَفْلَةِ، وَالْعَيْلَةِ، وَالذِّلَّةِ، وَالْمَسْكَنَةِ، وَالْكُفْرِ،
وَالْفُسُوْقِ، وَالشِّقَاقِ، وَالسُّمْعَةِ، وَالرِّيَاءِ، وَمِنَ
الصَّمَمِ، وَالْبَكَمِ، وَالْجُنُوْنِ، وَالْجُذَامِ، وَسَيِّئِ
الْأَسْقَامِ، وَضَلَعِ الدَّيْنِ، وَمِنَ الْهَمِّ، وَالْحَزَنِ،
وَالْبُخْلِ، وَغَلَبَةِ الرِّجَالِ، وَمِنْ أَنْ أُرَدَّ إِلٰى أَرْذَلِ
الْعُمُرِ، وَفِتْنَةِ الدُّنْيَا، وَمِنْ عِلْمٍ لَّا يَنْفَعُ، وَمِنْ
قَلْبٍ لَّا يَخْشَعُ، وَمِنْ نَّفْسٍ لَّا تَشْبَعُ، وَمِنْ دَعْوَةٍ
لَّا يُسْتَجَابُ لَهَا۔

SUNDAY

In the Name of Allah, the Most Compassionate, the Most Merciful

(55) *My Lord, help me and do not help my enemies against me. Aid me to victory and do not aid my enemies against me. Use Your plan for me and do not use Your plan against me. Guide me and make it easy for me to follow the guidance. Aid me to victory against those who act wrongfully toward me. My Lord, make me one who is most grateful to You, who constantly remembers You, who is full of fear toward You, who is fully obedient to You, who is humble before You, who is earnest in supplication to You, and who always turns to You. My Lord, accept my repentance, wash away my sin, grant my supplication, establish my evidence, make my speech upright, guide my heart, and throw out malice from my bosom.*

(56) *O Allah, forgive us. Have mercy on us. Be pleased with us. Accept from us. Admit us to Para-*

55 [ʿAbdullāh ibn ʿAbbās. *Sunan at-Tirmidhī* #3474]

56 [Abū Umāmah al-Bāhilī. *Sunan Ibn Mājah* #3826]

بِسْمِ اللَّهِ الرَّحْمَٰنِ الرَّحِيمِ

﴿٥٥﴾ رَبِّ أَعِنِّيْ وَلَا تُعِنْ عَلَيَّ، وَانْصُرْنِيْ وَلَا تَنْصُرْ عَلَيَّ، وَامْكُرْ لِيْ وَلَا تَمْكُرْ عَلَيَّ، وَاهْدِنِيْ وَيَسِّرْ لِيَ الْهُدٰى، وَانْصُرْنِيْ عَلٰى مَنْ بَغٰى عَلَيَّ. رَبِّ اجْعَلْنِيْ لَكَ شَكَّارًا، لَّكَ ذَكَّارًا، لَّكَ رَهَّابًا، لَّكَ مِطْوَاعًا، لَّكَ مُخْبِتًا، إِلَيْكَ أَوَّاهًا مُّنِيْبًا. رَبِّ تَقَبَّلْ تَوْبَتِيْ، وَاغْسِلْ حَوْبَتِيْ، وَأَجِبْ دَعْوَتِيْ، وَثَبِّتْ حُجَّتِيْ، وَسَدِّدْ لِسَانِيْ، وَاهْدِ قَلْبِيْ، وَاسْلُلْ سَخِيْمَةَ صَدْرِيْ۔

﴿٥٦﴾ اَللّٰهُمَّ اغْفِرْ لَنَا، وَارْحَمْنَا، وَارْضَ عَنَّا، وَتَقَبَّلْ مِنَّا، وَأَدْخِلْنَا الْجَنَّةَ، وَنَجِّنَا مِنَ النَّارِ،

dise and protect us from Hell. And set right all our affairs.

(57) O Allah, join our hearts, mend our relationships, and guide us to the paths of peace. Bring us out of darkness into light and keep us away from manifest and concealed obscenities. Bless us in our ears, our eyes, our hearts, our spouses, and our offspring. Accept our repentance. Indeed, You are the Most Forgiving, the Most Merciful. Make us grateful for Your blessings, so we receive them with due praise. And perfect them for us.

(58) O Allah, I beg You for steadfastness in religious affairs. I beg You for determination to follow the guidance. I beg You to enable me to show gratitude for Your bounties and to worship You with the best devotion. I beg You for a truthful tongue, a sound heart, and an upright character. I seek Your protection from the evil of all that only You are aware of. I beg You for the good that only You

57 [ʿAbdullāh ibn Masʿūd. *Sunan Abī Dāwūd* #825]

58 [Shaddād ibn ʾAws. *Sunan at-Tirmidhī* #3329; Ibid. *Mustadrak Ḥākim* #72/1872]

وَأَصْلِحْ لَنَا شَأْنَنَا كُلَّهُ.

﴿٥٧﴾ اَللّٰهُمَّ أَلِّفْ بَيْنَ قُلُوْبِنَا، وَأَصْلِحْ ذَاتَ بَيْنِنَا، وَاهْدِنَا سُبُلَ السَّلَامِ، وَنَجِّنَا مِنَ الظُّلُمَاتِ إِلَى النُّوْرِ، وَجَنِّبْنَا الْفَوَاحِشَ مَا ظَهَرَ مِنْهَا وَمَا بَطَنَ، وَبَارِكْ لَنَا فِيْ أَسْمَاعِنَا وَأَبْصَارِنَا وَقُلُوْبِنَا وَأَزْوَاجِنَا وَذُرِّيَّاتِنَا، وَتُبْ عَلَيْنَا، إِنَّكَ أَنْتَ التَّوَّابُ الرَّحِيْمُ، وَاجْعَلْنَا شَاكِرِيْنَ لِنِعْمَتِكَ، مُثْنِيْنَ بِهَا قَابِلِيْهَا، وَأَتِمَّهَا عَلَيْنَا.

﴿٥٨﴾ اَللّٰهُمَّ إِنِّيْ أَسْأَلُكَ الثَّبَاتَ فِي الْأَمْرِ، وَأَسْأَلُكَ عَزِيْمَةَ الرُّشْدِ، وَأَسْأَلُكَ شُكْرَ نِعْمَتِكَ، وَحُسْنَ عِبَادَتِكَ، وَأَسْأَلُكَ لِسَانًا صَادِقًا، وَقَلْبًا سَلِيْمًا، وَخُلُقًا مُسْتَقِيْمًا، وَأَعُوْذُ بِكَ مِنْ شَرِّ مَا

know. And I seek forgiveness from You for what You know (of my sins). Surely, You are the All-Knowing of the hidden.

(59) O Allah, forgive what I did earlier and what I delayed; what I did secretly and what I did publicly; and whatever you know more than I.

(60) O Allah, grant us that fear of You by which You may come between us and our disobedience to You. Grant us that obedience to You with which You may lead us to Paradise. Give us that faith with which You will lighten the worldly hardships for us. Grant us the use of our ears, eyes, and other faculties as long as You keep us alive. And make these our survivors. Make our revenge target (only) those who oppress us. Help us to victory over the one who displays enmity to us. Do not let our misfortunes hit our religion. Do not make this world our greatest concern and the sum total of our knowledge. And do not impose over us one who shows no mercy to us.

---

59 [ʿAbdullāh ibn ʿUmar. *Mustadrak Ḥākim* #134/1934]

60 [ʿAbdullāh ibn ʿUmar. *Riyāḍ aṣ-Ṣāliḥīn* #834; *Sunan at-Tirmidhī* #3434]

تَعْلَمُ، وَأَسْأَلُكَ مِنْ خَيْرِ مَا تَعْلَمُ، وَأَسْتَغْفِرُكَ مِمَّا تَعْلَمُ، إِنَّكَ أَنْتَ عَلَّامُ الْغُيُوْبِ.

﴿٥٩﴾ اَللّٰهُمَّ اغْفِرْ لِيْ مَا قَدَّمْتُ وَمَا أَخَّرْتُ، وَمَا أَسْرَرْتُ وَمَا أَعْلَنْتُ، وَمَا أَنْتَ أَعْلَمُ بِهٖ مِنِّيْ.

﴿٦٠﴾ اَللّٰهُمَّ اقْسِمْ لَنَا مِنْ خَشْيَتِكَ مَا تَحُوْلُ بِهٖ بَيْنَنَا وَبَيْنَ مَعَاصِيْكَ، وَمِنْ طَاعَتِكَ مَا تُبَلِّغُنَا بِهٖ جَنَّتَكَ، وَمِنَ الْيَقِيْنِ مَا تُهَوِّنُ بِهٖ عَلَيْنَا مَصَائِبَ الدُّنْيَا، وَمَتِّعْنَا بِأَسْمَاعِنَا وَأَبْصَارِنَا وَقُوَّاتِنَا مَا أَحْيَيْتَنَا، وَاجْعَلْهُ الْوَارِثَ مِنَّا، وَاجْعَلْ ثَأْرَنَا عَلٰى مَنْ ظَلَمَنَا، وَانْصُرْنَا عَلٰى مَنْ عَادَانَا، وَلَا تَجْعَلْ مُصِيْبَتَنَا فِيْ دِيْنِنَا، وَلَا تَجْعَلِ الدُّنْيَا أَكْبَرَ هَمِّنَا، وَلَا مَبْلَغَ عِلْمِنَا، وَلَا تُسَلِّطْ عَلَيْنَا مَنْ لَّا يَرْحَمُنَا.

(61) O Allah, increase (Your grace) for us and do not curtail it; give us honor and do not humiliate us; give us and do not deprive us; favor us and do not favor others over us; make us be pleased with You and be pleased with us.

(62) O Allah, inspire me with the right guidance for me.

(63) O Allah, protect me from the evil of my self and give me the determination to do what is most right in my affairs.

(64) O Allah, I beg You for well-being in this world and in the Hereafter.

(65) O Allah, I beg You to enable me to do good deeds, to shun bad deeds, and to love the poor. (I beg You to) forgive me and have mercy on me. And when You plan tribulations for a people cause me

61 ['Umar ibn al-Khaṭṭāb. *Sunan at-Tirmidhī* #3097]

62 ['Imrān ibn Ḥuṣayn. *Sunan at-Tirmidhī* #3405]

63 ['Imrān ibn Ḥuṣayn. *Musnad Aḥmad* #19141]

64 [Abū Hurayrah. *Kanz al-'Ummāl* #3201]

65 [Mu'ādh ibn Jabal. *Sunan at-Tirmidhī* #3159; Thawbān ibn Bajdad. *Mustadrak Ḥākim* #132/1932]

﴿٦١﴾ اَللّٰهُمَّ زِدْنَا وَلَا تَنْقُصْنَا، وَأَكْرِمْنَا وَلَا تُهِنَّا، وَأَعْطِنَا وَلَا تَحْرِمْنَا، وَاٰثِرْنَا وَلَا تُؤْثِرْ عَلَيْنَا، وَأَرْضِنَا وَارْضَ عَنَّا۔

﴿٦٢﴾ اَللّٰهُمَّ أَلْهِمْنِيْ رُشْدِيْ۔

﴿٦٣﴾ اَللّٰهُمَّ قِنِيْ شَرَّ نَفْسِيْ وَاعْزِمْ لِيْ عَلٰى أَرْشَدِ أَمْرِيْ۔

﴿٦٤﴾ اَللّٰهُمَّ إِنِّيْ أَسْأَلُكَ الْعَافِيَةَ فِي الدُّنْيَا وَالْاٰخِرَةِ۔

﴿٦٥﴾ اَللّٰهُمَّ إِنِّيْ أَسْأَلُكَ فِعْلَ الْخَيْرَاتِ، وَتَرْكَ الْمُنْكَرَاتِ، وَحُبَّ الْمَسَاكِيْنِ، وَأَنْ تَغْفِرَ لِيْ وَتَرْحَمَنِيْ، وَإِذَا أَرَدْتَّ بِقَوْمٍ فِتْنَةً فَتَوَفَّنِيْ غَيْرَ

to die without being put to trial. I beg for Your love, and the love of the one who loves You, and the love of such deeds that will bring me closer to Your love.

(66) *O Allah, make Your love dearer to me than myself, my family, and cold water.*

(67) *O Allah, provide me with Your love and the love of those whose love will benefit me with You. O Allah, whatever you provided to me of the things that I love, make them a source of strength for me in pursuing what You love. O Allah, and whatever you kept away from me of the things that I crave, make their absence free up time that I can devote to whatever You love.*

(68) *O Turner of hearts, keep my heart steadfast on Your religion.*

---

66 [Abū ad-Dardā'. *Sunan at-Tirmidhī* #3412]

67 [ʿAbdullāh ibn Yazīd al-Khaṭamī al-Anṣārī. *Sunan at-Tirmidhī* #3413]

68 [Anas ibn Mālik. *Sunan at-Tirmidhī* #2066]

مَفْتُوْنٍ، وَّأَسْأَلُكَ حُبَّكَ وَحُبَّ مَنْ يُّحِبُّكَ، وَحُبَّ عَمَلٍ يُّقَرِّبُنِيْ إِلىٰ حُبِّكَ۔

﴿٦٦﴾ اَللّٰهُمَّ اجْعَلْ حُبَّكَ أَحَبَّ إِلَيَّ مِنْ نَّفْسِيْ وَأَهْلِيْ وَمِنَ الْمَاءِ الْبَارِدِ۔

﴿٦٧﴾ اَللّٰهُمَّ ارْزُقْنِيْ حُبَّكَ وَحُبَّ مَنْ يَّنْفَعُنِيْ حُبُّهٗ عِنْدَكَ. اَللّٰهُمَّ مَا رَزَقْتَنِيْ مِمَّا أُحِبُّ فَاجْعَلْهُ قُوَّةً لِّيْ فِيْمَا تُحِبُّ. اَللّٰهُمَّ وَمَا زَوَيْتَ عَنِّيْ مِمَّا أُحِبُّ فَاجْعَلْهُ فَرَاغًا لِّيْ فِيْمَا تُحِبُّ۔

﴿٦٨﴾ يَا مُقَلِّبَ الْقُلُوْبِ ثَبِّتْ قَلْبِيْ عَلىٰ دِيْنِكَ۔

(69) O Allah, I beg You for the faith that will not be shaken, the blessings that will not end, and the company of our Prophet Muḥammad ﷺ in the highest section of the eternal Paradise.

(70) O Allah, I ask You for sound health with faith, faith with good manners, success here followed by success in the Hereafter, mercy from You, health and safety, and Your forgiveness and pleasure.

(71) O Allah, cause me to benefit from what You have taught me and teach me what will benefit me.

(72) O Allah, with Your knowledge of the unseen, and Your absolute power over the creations, let me live in this world as long as You know my living is good for me, and give me death when You know death is better for me. I beg You for Your fear in

---

69 [ʿAbdullāh ibn Masʿūd. *Kanz al-ʿUmmāl* #5088; Ibid. *Mustadrak Ḥākim* #128/1928]

70 [Abū Hurayrah. *Mustadrak Ḥākim* #119/1919]

71 [Anas ibn Mālik. *Mustadrak Ḥākim* #79/1879]

72 [ʿAmmār ibn Yāsir. *Sunan an-Nasāʾī* #1289]

﴿٦٩﴾ اَللّٰهُمَّ إِنِّيْ أَسْأَلُكَ إِيْمَانًا لَّا يَرْتَدُّ وَنَعِيْمًا لَّا يَنْفَدُ وَمُرَافَقَةَ نَبِيِّنَا مُحَمَّدٍ صَلَّى اللهُ عَلَيْهِ وَسَلَّمَ فِيْ أَعْلٰى دَرَجَةِ الْجَنَّةِ جَنَّةِ الْخُلْدِ۔

﴿٧٠﴾ اَللّٰهُمَّ إِنِّيْ أَسْأَلُكَ صِحَّةً فِيْ إِيْمَانٍ، وَّإِيْمَانًا فِيْ حُسْنِ خُلُقٍ، وَّنَجَاحًا يَّتْبَعُهُ فَلَاحٌ، وَّرَحْمَةً مِّنْكَ وَعَافِيَةً، وَّمَغْفِرَةً مِّنْكَ وَرِضْوَانًا۔

﴿٧١﴾ اَللّٰهُمَّ انْفَعْنِيْ بِمَا عَلَّمْتَنِيْ وَعَلِّمْنِيْ مَا يَنْفَعُنِيْ۔

﴿٧٢﴾ اَللّٰهُمَّ بِعِلْمِكَ الْغَيْبَ وَقُدْرَتِكَ عَلَى الْخَلْقِ أَحْيِنِيْ مَا عَلِمْتَ الْحَيٰوةَ خَيْرًا لِّيْ، وَتَوَفَّنِيْ إِذَا عَلِمْتَ الْوَفَاةَ خَيْرًا لِّيْ. وَأَسْأَلُكَ خَشْيَتَكَ فِيْ

secret and in public and sincere talk in times of joy and anger. I beg You for endless blessings and perpetual comfort of my eyes. I beg You that I become pleased with fate. (I beg You) for a cool, comfortable life after death; the delight of the sight of Your Countenance (after death); and the longing to meet You (before death). I seek Your protection against deeply hurting ordeals and tribulations that lead one astray. O Allah, adorn us with the beauty of faith and make us properly guided guides for other people.

(73) O Allah, I beg You for all the good, immediate and in the future; that of which I know and that of which I know not.

(74) O Allah, I beg You for every good that Your servant and prophet ﷺ asked You for. O Allah, I beg You for Paradise and all words or actions that may bring me close to it. I beg You that You make

---

73 [ʿĀ'ishah. *Sunan Ibn Mājah* #3836]

74 [ʿĀ'ishah. *Sunan Ibn Mājah* #3836; Ibid. *Mustadrak Ḥākim* #114/1914]

الْغَيْبِ وَالشَّهَادَةِ، وَكَلِمَةَ الْإِخْلَاصِ فِي الرِّضٰى وَالْغَضَبِ. وَأَسْأَلُكَ نَعِيمًا لَّا يَنْفَدُ، وَقُرَّةَ عَيْنٍ لَّا تَنْقَطِعُ، وَأَسْأَلُكَ الرِّضَاءَ بِالْقَضَاءِ، وَبَرْدَ الْعَيْشِ بَعْدَ الْمَوْتِ، وَلَذَّةَ النَّظَرِ إِلٰى وَجْهِكَ، وَالشَّوْقَ إِلٰى لِقَائِكَ، وَأَعُوْذُ بِكَ مِنْ ضَرَّاءَ مُضِرَّةٍ وَّفِتْنَةٍ مُّضِلَّةٍ. اَللّٰهُمَّ زَيِّنَّا بِزِيْنَةِ الْإِيْمَانِ، وَاجْعَلْنَا هُدَاةً مُّهْتَدِيْنَ۔

﴿٧٣﴾ اَللّٰهُمَّ إِنِّيْ أَسْأَلُكَ مِنَ الْخَيْرِ كُلِّهٖ، عَاجِلِهٖ وَاٰجِلِهٖ، مَا عَلِمْتُ مِنْهُ وَمَا لَمْ أَعْلَمْ۔

﴿٧٤﴾ اَللّٰهُمَّ إِنِّيْ أَسْأَلُكَ مِنْ خَيْرِ مَا سَأَلَكَ عَبْدُكَ وَنَبِيُّكَ. اَللّٰهُمَّ إِنِّيْ أَسْأَلُكَ الْجَنَّةَ وَمَا قَرَّبَ إِلَيْهَا مِنْ قَوْلٍ أَوْ عَمَلٍ، وَّأَسْأَلُكَ أَنْ تَجْعَلَ كُلَّ

every decree of fate good for me. And I beg You that whatever decisions You make for me, make their end good.

(75) O Allah, make the end of all our affairs the best and save us from disgrace in this world and punishment in the Hereafter.

(76) O Allah, protect me with Islam while I am standing, protect me with Islam while I am sitting, and protect me with Islam while I am lying down. And let not an enemy or a jealous person take delight from my plight. O Allah, I ask You for all the good whose treasures are in Your Hands, and I ask You for that good which is totally in Your Hands.

(77) O Allah, do not leave any of our sins except that you forgive them, nor any of our worries except that you remove them, nor any of our debts except that you discharge them, nor any of our needs from this world and the Hereafter except that you

75 [Busr ibn Arṭāt al-Qurashī. *Musnad Aḥmad* #16970]

76 [Composite: ʿAbdullāh ibn Masʿūd. *Kanz al-ʿUmmāl* #3679; ʿUmar ibn al-Khaṭṭāb. *Kanz al-ʿUmmāl* #5035]

77 [Anas ibn Mālik. *Majmaʿ az-Zawā'id* #17266]

قَضَاءٍ قَضَيْتَهُ لِيْ خَيْرًا، وَّأَسْأَلُكَ مَا قَضَيْتَ لِيْ مِنْ أَمْرٍ أَنْ تَجْعَلَ عَاقِبَتَهُ رُشْدًا۔

﴿٧٥﴾ اَللّٰهُمَّ أَحْسِنْ عَاقِبَتَنَا فِي الْأُمُوْرِ كُلِّهَا، وَأَجِرْنَا مِنْ خِزْيِ الدُّنْيَا وَعَذَابِ الْاٰخِرَةِ۔

﴿٧٦﴾ اَللّٰهُمَّ احْفَظْنِيْ بِالْإِسْلَامِ قَائِمًا، وَّاحْفَظْنِيْ بِالْإِسْلَامِ قَاعِدًا، وَّاحْفَظْنِيْ بِالْإِسْلَامِ رَاقِدًا، وَّلَا تُشْمِتْ بِيْ عَدُوًّا وَّلَا حَاسِدًا. اَللّٰهُمَّ إِنِّيْ أَسْأَلُكَ مِنْ كُلِّ خَيْرٍ خَزَائِنُهُ بِيَدِكَ۔ وَأَسْأَلُكَ مِنَ الْخَيْرِ الَّذِيْ هُوَ بِيَدِكَ كُلِّهٖ۔

﴿٧٧﴾ اَللّٰهُمَّ لَا تَدَعْ لَنَا ذَنْبًا إِلَّا غَفَرْتَهُ، وَلَا هَمًّا إِلَّا فَرَّجْتَهُ، وَلَا دَيْنًا إِلَّا قَضَيْتَهُ، وَلَا حَاجَةً مِّنْ حَوَائِجِ

satisfy them. O the Most Merciful of the merciful.

(78) O Allah, help us in Your remembrance, in gratitude to You, and in reaching excellence in Your worship.

(79) O Allah, make me content with what You have provided for me and bless me in it, and be my protector in everything that is out of my sight.

(80) O Allah, I ask You for a clean life, a graceful death, and a return (to You) which is neither humiliating nor disgracing.

(81) O Allah, I am weak; replace my weakness with strength in my pursuits of Your pleasure. Pull me by my forelocks toward good. Make Islam the ultimate object of my pleasure. I am lowly, so give me honor. And I am needy, so provide for me.

---

78 [Abū Hurayrah. *Kanz al-ʿUmmāl* #3700; Muʿādh ibn Jabal. *Sunan Abī Dāwūd* #1301]

79 [ʿAbdullāh ibn ʿAbbās. *Mustadrak Ḥākim* #78/1878]

80 [ʿAbdullāh ibn ʿUmar. *Mustadrak Ḥākim* #186/1986]

81 [Buraydah al-Aslamī. *Mustadrak Ḥākim* #131/1931; Ibid. *Al-Jāmiʿ aṣ-Ṣaghīr* #2882]

الدُّنْيَا وَالْاٰخِرَةِ إِلَّا قَضَيْتَهَا، يَا أَرْحَمَ الرَّاحِمِيْنَ۔

﴿٧٨﴾ اَللّٰهُمَّ أَعِنَّا عَلٰى ذِكْرِكَ وَشُكْرِكَ وَحُسْنِ عِبَادَتِكَ۔

﴿٧٩﴾ اَللّٰهُمَّ قَنِّعْنِيْ بِمَا رَزَقْتَنِيْ وَبَارِكْ لِيْ فِيْهِ، وَاخْلُفْ عَلٰى كُلِّ غَائِبَةٍ لِّيْ بِخَيْرٍ۔

﴿٨٠﴾ اَللّٰهُمَّ إِنِّيْ أَسْأَلُكَ عِيْشَةً نَّقِيَّةً، وَّمِيْتَةً سَوِيَّةً، وَّمَرَدًّا غَيْرَ مُخْزِيٍّ وَّلَا فَاضِحٍ۔

﴿٨١﴾ اَللّٰهُمَّ إِنِّيْ ضَعِيْفٌ فَقَوِّ فِيْ رِضَاكَ ضُعْفِيْ، وَخُذْ إِلَى الْخَيْرِ بِنَاصِيَتِيْ، وَاجْعَلِ الْإِسْلَامَ مُنْتَهٰى رِضَائِيْ، وَإِنِّيْ ذَلِيْلٌ فَأَعِزَّنِيْ، وَإِنِّيْ فَقِيْرٌ فَارْزُقْنِيْ۔

(82) O Allah, I beg You for the best of petitions and invocations, thorough success, best deeds, best recompense, best life, and best death. Grant me firmness. Make my scales heavy and my faith genuine. Elevate my ranks, accept my ṣalāh, and forgive my sins. I ask of You high ranks in Paradise. Āmīn. O Allah, I beg You for the good: its beginnings and endings, its most comprehensive forms, its first and its last, and its outward and inward manifestations. O Allah, I beg You for the good of my accomplishments, my deeds, and my actions. The good of that which is hidden and that which is exposed.

(83) O Allah, make my sustenance the most plentiful in my old age and during the last days of my life.

---

82 [Um Salamah. *Kanz al-ʿUmmāl* #3820; Ibid. *Mustadrak Ḥākim* #111/1911]

83 [ʿĀʾishah. *Mustadrak Ḥākim* #187/1987]

﴿٨٢﴾ اَللّٰهُمَّ إِنِّيْ أَسْأَلُكَ خَيْرَ الْمَسْأَلَةِ، وَخَيْرَ الدُّعَاءِ، وَخَيْرَ النَّجَاحِ، وَخَيْرَ الْعَمَلِ، وَخَيْرَ الثَّوَابِ، وَخَيْرَ الْحَيٰوةِ، وَخَيْرَ الْمَمَاتِ، وَثَبِّتْنِيْ، وَثَقِّلْ مَوَازِيْنِيْ، وَحَقِّقْ إِيْمَانِيْ، وَارْفَعْ دَرَجَاتِيْ، وَتَقَبَّلْ صَلَاتِيْ، وَاغْفِرْ خَطِيْئَتِيْ، وَأَسْأَلُكَ الدَّرَجَاتِ الْعُلٰى مِنَ الْجَنَّةِ، اٰمِيْنَ. اَللّٰهُمَّ إِنِّيْ أَسْأَلُكَ فَوَاتِحَ الْخَيْرِ وَخَوَاتِمَهٗ، وَجَوَامِعَهٗ، وَأَوَّلَهٗ وَاٰخِرَهٗ، وَظَاهِرَهٗ وَبَاطِنَهٗ. اَللّٰهُمَّ إِنِّيْ أَسْأَلُكَ خَيْرَ مَا اٰتِيْ، وَخَيْرَ مَا أَفْعَلُ، وَخَيْرَ مَا أَعْمَلُ، وَخَيْرَ مَا بَطَنَ، وَخَيْرَ مَا ظَهَرَ۔

﴿٨٣﴾ اَللّٰهُمَّ اجْعَلْ أَوْسَعَ رِزْقِكَ عَلَيَّ عِنْدَ كِبَرِ سِنِّيْ وَانْقِطَاعِ عُمُرِيْ۔

(84) O Allah, make the last part of my life its best, my last deed my best one, and the day I meet You my best day. O Protector of Islam and its followers, keep me firm on it until I meet you. I seek from You my contentment and that of my family.

(85) O Allah, I seek Your protection from undesirable age and mischief of the heart. I seek Your refuge, by virtue of Your Honor as there is no god except You, from that You should lead me astray. (I seek Your refuge) from severe trials, wretchedness, bad fate, and taunts from the enemies. From the evil of what I did and what I did not. From the loss of Your blessings and the removal of Your protection. From Your sudden punishment and from all (that can warrant) Your wrath. From the mischief of my hearing, sight, speech, heart, and seed.

84 [Composite: Anas ibn Mālik. *Majma' az-Zawā'id* #17267; Abū Ṣirmah. *Musnad Aḥmad* #15194]

85 [Composite: 'Umar ibn al-Khaṭṭāb. *Sunan an-Nasā'ī* #5402; 'Abdullāh ibn 'Abbās. *Ṣaḥīḥ Muslim* #4894; Abū Hurayrah. *Ṣaḥīḥ al-Bukhārī* #5871; 'Ā'ishah. *Ṣaḥīḥ Muslim* #4891; 'Abdullāh ibn 'Umar. *Ṣaḥīḥ Muslim* #4922; Shakal ibn Ḥumayd. *Sunan at-Tirmidhī* #3414; Abū Hurayrah. *Kanz al-'Ummāl* #3688; Abul-Yasr. *Sunan Abī Dāwūd* #1328]

﴿٨٤﴾ وَاجْعَلْ خَيْرَ عُمُرِيْ اٰخِرَهٗ، وَخَيْرَ عَمَلِيْ خَوَاتِيْمَهٗ، وَخَيْرَ أَيَّامِيْ يَوْمَ أَلْقَاكَ فِيْهِ. يَا وَلِيَّ الْإِسْلَامِ وَأَهْلِهٖ ثَبِّتْنِيْ بِهٖ حَتّٰى أَلْقَاكَ ـ أَسْأَلُكَ غِنَايَ وَغِنٰى مَوْلَايَ ـ

﴿٨٥﴾ اَللّٰهُمَّ إِنِّيْ أَعُوْذُ بِكَ مِنْ سُوْءِ الْعُمُرِ وَفِتْنَةِ الصَّدْرِ، وَأَعُوْذُ بِعِزَّتِكَ لَا إِلٰهَ إِلَّا أَنْتَ أَنْ تُضِلَّنِيْ، وَمِنْ جَهْدِ الْبَلَاءِ، وَدَرَكِ الشَّقَاءِ، وَسُوْءِ الْقَضَاءِ، وَشَمَاتَةِ الْأَعْدَاءِ، وَمِنْ شَرِّ مَا عَمِلْتُ، وَمِنْ شَرِّ مَا لَمْ أَعْمَلْ، وَمِنْ زَوَالِ نِعْمَتِكَ، وَتَحَوُّلِ عَافِيَتِكَ، وَفُجَاءَةِ نِقْمَتِكَ، وَجَمِيْعِ سَخَطِكَ، وَمِنْ شَرِّ سَمْعِيْ، وَمِنْ شَرِّ بَصَرِيْ، وَمِنْ شَرِّ لِسَانِيْ، وَمِنْ شَرِّ قَلْبِيْ، وَمِنْ شَرِّ مَنِيِّيْ، وَمِنْ أَنْ أَظْلِمَ

From oppressing others or being oppressed, from being crushed, from a fatal fall, from drowning or being burnt. Or that Shayṭān should confuse me at the time of my death. Or that I should die as a fugitive from jihad or that I should die due to a venomous bite.

أَوْ أُظْلَمَ، وَمِنَ الْهَدَمِ، وَمِنَ التَّرَدِّيْ، وَمِنَ الْغَرَقِ وَالْحَرَقِ، وَأَنْ يَتَخَبَّطَنِيَ الشَّيْطَانُ عِنْدَ الْمَوْتِ، وَمِنْ أَنْ أَمُوْتَ فِيْ سَبِيْلِكَ مُدْبِرًا، وَأَنْ أَمُوْتَ لَدِيْغًا.

MONDAY

In the Name of Allah, the Most Compassionate, the Most Merciful

(86) O Allah, make me one who is highly grateful. Make me one who is patient and perseverant. Make me small in my own eyes but great in the eyes of others.

(87) O Allah, put blessings, beauty, and calm in our land. Do not deprive me of the blessings of what You have given me and do not subject me to a trial in what You have withheld from me.

(88) O Allah, You have given me a good physique; favor me with good morals and manners as well. Extinguish the anger in my heart and, as long as You keep me alive, save me from such trying situations that can lead me astray.

---

86 [Buraydah al-Aslamī. *Kanz al-ʿUmmāl* #3675]

87 [Composite: Samurah ibn Jundub and Ubayy ibn Kaʿb. *Majmaʿ az-Zawāʾid* #17425, 17359]

88 [Composite: ʿAbdullāh ibn Masʿūd. *Musnad Aḥmad* #3632; Um Salamah. *Musnad Aḥmad* #25364]

بِسْمِ اللَّهِ الرَّحْمَنِ الرَّحِيمِ

﴿٨٦﴾ اَللّٰهُمَّ اجْعَلْنِيْ شَكُوْرًا، وَّاجْعَلْنِيْ صَبُوْرًا، وَّاجْعَلْنِيْ فِيْ عَيْنِيْ صَغِيْرًا، وَّفِيْ أَعْيُنِ النَّاسِ كَبِيْرًا۔

﴿٨٧﴾ اَللّٰهُمَّ ضَعْ فِيْ أَرْضِنَا بَرَكَتَهَا وَزِيْنَتَهَا وَسَكَنَهَا۔ وَلَا تَحْرِمْنِيْ بَرَكَةَ مَا أَعْطَيْتَنِيْ، وَلَا تَفْتِنِّيْ فِيْمَا أَحْرَمْتَنِيْ۔

﴿٨٨﴾ اَللّٰهُمَّ أَحْسَنْتَ خَلْقِيْ فَأَحْسِنْ خُلُقِيْ۔ وَأَذْهِبْ غَيْظَ قَلْبِيْ، وَأَجِرْنِيْ مِنْ مُّضِلَّاتِ الْفِتَنِ مَا أَحْيَيْتَنَا۔

(89) O Allah, instruct me in the evidence of faith at the time of death.

(90) O Lord, I beg You for the good of this day and the good of what will come after it.

(91) O Allah, I beseech You for the good of this day: its victory, its success, its light, its blessing, and its guidance.

(92) O Allah, I ask You for forgiveness and security in my religion and in my worldly affairs, in my family and in my property. O Allah, conceal those things of mine that are worth concealing and give calm to my fears. O Allah, guard me (from all sides): in front and behind, on my right and on my left, and from above me. And I seek refuge in Your greatness from receiving unexpected harm from below.

---

89 [Abū Hurayrah. *Kanz al-ʿUmmāl* #3286]

90 [ʿAbdullāh ibn Masʿūd. *Sunan at-Tirmidhī* #3312]

91 [Abū Mālik al-Ashʿarī. *Sunan Abī Dāwūd* #4421]

92 [ʿAbdullāh ibn ʿUmar. *Sunan Abī Dāwūd* #4412]

﴿٨٩﴾ اَللّٰهُمَّ لَقِّنِي حُجَّةَ الْإِيمَانِ عِنْدَ الْمَمَاتِ۔

﴿٩٠﴾ رَبِّ أَسْأَلُكَ خيْرَ مَا فِيْ هٰذَا الْيَوْمِ وَخَيْرَ مَا بَعْدَهٗ۔

﴿٩١﴾ اَللّٰهُمَّ إِنِّيْ أَسْأَلُكَ خيْرَ هٰذَا الْيَوْمِ فَتْحَهٗ وَنَصْرَهٗ وَنُوْرَهٗ وَبَرَكَتَهٗ وَهُدَاهُ۔

﴿٩٢﴾ اَللّٰهُمَّ إِنِّيْ أَسْأَلُكَ الْعَفْوَ وَالْعَافِيَةَ فِيْ دِيْنِي وَدُنْيَايَ وَأَهْلِيْ وَمَالِيْ. اَللّٰهُمَّ اسْتُرْ عَوْرَاتِيْ وَاٰمِنْ رَوْعَاتِيْ. اَللّٰهُمَّ احْفَظْنِيْ مِنْ بَيْنِ يَدَيَّ وَمِنْ خَلْفِيْ، وَعَنْ يَّمِيْنِيْ وَعَنْ شِمَالِيْ، وَمِنْ فَوْقِيْ، وَأَعُوْذُ بِعَظَمَتِكَ أَنْ أُغْتَالَ مِنْ تَحْتِيْ۔

(93) O the Living, the Eternal, I beg through Your mercy. Set right all of my affairs and do not leave me under the control of my ego (nafs) for even the blink of an eye.

(94) In the name of the light of Your Countenance that lights the heavens and the earth and in the name of every right of Yours and (in the name of) the right on You that You have granted to the beggars, I beseech You to forgive me and protect me from the Fire through Your Power.

(95) O Allah, make the first part of this day good, the middle part success, and the last part salvation. I ask from You the good of this world and the Hereafter, O the Most Merciful of the merciful.

(96) O Allah, forgive me my sins, expel my Shayṭān, and redeem my pledge (settle for me my

---

93 [Anas ibn Mālik. *Mustadrak Ḥākim* #200/2000]

94 [Abū Umāmah al-Bāhilī. *Muʿjam al-Kabīr (Ṭabarānī)* #265/8]

95 [ʿAbdur-Raḥmān ibn Abzā. *Muṣannaf ibn Abī Shaybah* #29268]

96 [Abū al-Azhar al-Anmārī. *Sunan Abī Dāwūd* #4395; Ibid. *Mustadrak Ḥākim* #182/1982]

﴿٩٣﴾ يَا حَيُّ يَا قَيُّوْمُ بِرَحْمَتِكَ أَسْتَغِيْثُ، أَصْلِحْ لِيْ شَأْنِيْ كُلَّهُ، وَلَا تَكِلْنِيْ إِلٰى نَفْسِيْ طَرْفَةَ عَيْنٍ۔

﴿٩٤﴾ أَسْأَلُكَ بِنُوْرِ وَجْهِكَ الَّذِيْ أَشْرَقَتْ لَهُ السَّمٰوٰتُ وَالأَرْضُ وَبِكُلِّ حَقٍّ هُوَ لَكَ وَبِحَقِّ السَّائِلِيْنَ عَلَيْكَ أَنْ تُقِيْلَنِيْ وَأَنْ تُجِيْرَنِيْ مِنَ النَّارِ بِقُدْرَتِكَ۔

﴿٩٥﴾ اَللّٰهُمَّ اجْعَلْ أَوَّلَ هٰذَا النَّهَارِ صَلَاحًا، وَّأَوْسَطَهُ فَلَاحًا، وَّاٰخِرَهُ نَجَاحًا. أَسْأَلُكَ خَيْرَ الدُّنْيَا وَالْاٰخِرَةِ، يَا أَرْحَمَ الرَّاحِمِيْنَ۔

﴿٩٦﴾ اَللّٰهُمَّ اغْفِرْ لِيْ ذَنْبِيْ، وَاخْسِئْ شَيْطَانِيْ، وَفُكَّ رِهَانِيْ، وَثَقِّلْ مِيْزَانِيْ، وَاجْعَلْنِيْ فِي النَّدِيِّ

debts). Make my scales heavy and enter me into the Highest Council.

(97) O Allah, save me from Your punishment on the day You raise Your servants to life again.

(98) O Allah, Lord of the seven heavens and whatever comes under their shadows. Lord of the earths and whatever they bear. Lord of the devils and whatever they mislead. Be a Protector for me from the mischiefs of Your entire creation lest any of them do evil or oppress me. Strong is Your protection and blessed is Your name.

(99) There is no god except You, You have no partner. Glorified are You, O Allah, I seek forgiveness from You for my sin and I beseech You for Your mercy.

(100) O Allah, forgive my sin, make my home ample for me, and bless me in my sustenance.

---

97 [Ḥafṣah. *Sunan Abī Dāwūd* #4388]

98 [Khālid ibn al-Walīd. *Majmaʿ az-Zawā'id* #17063]

99 [ʿĀ'ishah. *Kanz al-ʿUmmāl* #23417]

100 [Abū Hurayrah. *Kanz al-ʿUmmāl* #3633]

الْأَعْلٰى۔

﴿٩٧﴾ اَللّٰهُمَّ قِنِي عَذَابَكَ يَوْمَ تَبْعَثُ عِبَادَكَ۔

﴿٩٨﴾ اَللّٰهُمَّ رَبَّ السَّمٰوٰتِ السَّبْعِ وَمَا أَظَلَّتْ، وَرَبَّ الْأَرَضِيْنَ وَمَا أَقَلَّتْ، وَرَبَّ الشَّيَاطِيْنِ وَمَا أَضَلَّتْ، كُنْ لِّيْ جَارًا مِّنْ شَرِّ خَلْقِكَ أَجْمَعِيْنَ أَنْ يَّفْرُطَ عَلَيَّ أَحَدٌ مِّنْهُمْ أَوْ أَنْ يَّطْغٰى، عَزَّ جَارُكَ وَتَبَارَكَ اسْمُكَ۔

﴿٩٩﴾ لَا إِلٰهَ إِلَّا أَنْتَ لَا شَرِيْكَ لَكَ سُبْحَانَكَ. اَللّٰهُمَّ إِنِّيْ أَسْتَغْفِرُكَ لِذَنْبِيْ وَأَسْأَلُكَ رَحْمَتَكَ۔

﴿١٠٠﴾ اَللّٰهُمَّ اغْفِرْ لِيْ ذَنْبِيْ، وَوَسِّعْ لِيْ فِيْ دَارِيْ، وَبَارِكْ لِيْ فِيْ رِزْقِيْ۔

(101) *O Allah, make me one of those who turn to You and repent much, and make me one of those who stay very clean and very pure.*

(102) *O Allah, forgive me, guide me, provide for me, and give me protection. And guide me with Your Will to the right thing in whatever is controversial.*

(103) *O Allah, put Light in my heart, Light in my sight, Light in my hearing, Light to my right, Light to my left, Light behind me, and Light in front of me. (O Allah,) bestow upon me Light. (O Allah,) put Light in my muscles, Light in my flesh, Light in my blood, Light in my hair, Light in my skin, Light in my tongue, and Light in my soul. Make my Light great and make me all Light.*

---

101 [ʿUmar ibn al-Khaṭṭāb. *Sunan at-Tirmidhī* #50]

102 [Composite: ʿĀ'ishah. *Sunan an-Nasā'ī* #5440; Ibid. *Ṣaḥīḥ Muslim* #1289]

103 [ʿAbdullāh ibn ʿAbbās. *Ṣaḥīḥ al-Bukhārī* #5841; *Ṣaḥīḥ Muslim* #1279]

﴿١٠١﴾ اَللّٰهُمَّ اجْعَلْنِيْ مِنَ التَّوَّابِيْنَ وَاجْعَلْنِيْ مِنَ الْمُتَطَهِّرِيْنَ۔

﴿١٠٢﴾ اَللّٰهُمَّ اغْفِرْ لِيْ، وَاهْدِنِيْ، وَارْزُقْنِيْ، وَعَافِنِيْ، وَاهْدِنِيْ لِمَا اخْتُلِفَ فِيْهِ مِنَ الْحَقِّ بِإِذْنِكَ۔

﴿١٠٣﴾ اَللّٰهُمَّ اجْعَلْ فِيْ قَلْبِيْ نُوْرًا، وَّفِيْ بَصَرِيْ نُوْرًا، وَّفِيْ سَمْعِيْ نُوْرًا، وَّعَنْ يَّمِيْنِيْ نُوْرًا، وَّعَنْ شِمَالِيْ نُوْرًا، وَّخَلْفِيْ نُوْرًا، وَّمِنْ أَمَامِيْ نُوْرًا، وَّاجْعَلْ لِّيْ نُوْرًا، وَّفِيْ عَصَبِيْ نُوْرًا، وَّفِيْ لَحْمِيْ نُوْرًا، وَّفِيْ دَمِيْ نُوْرًا، وَّفِيْ شَعْرِيْ نُوْرًا، وَّفِيْ بَشَرِيْ نُوْرًا، وَّفِيْ لِسَانِيْ نُوْرًا، وَّاجْعَلْ فِيْ نَفْسِيْ نُوْرًا، وَّأَعْظِمْ لِيْ نُوْرًا، وَّاجْعَلْنِيْ نُوْرًا، وَّاجْعَلْ

And put Light above me and Light below me. O Allah, give me Light.

(104) O Allah, open for us the doors to Your mercy and give us easy access to the doors to Your provisions.

(105) O Allah, protect me from the cursed Shayṭān.

(106) O Allah, I beg You for Your favor.

(107) O Allah, forgive all of my sins and mistakes. O Allah, elevate me, give me life and provisions, and guide me to pious deeds and morals. Certainly no one leads to the pious deeds and morals and no one protects from the evil ones except You.

(108) O Allah, I beg You for provisions that are pure, knowledge that is beneficial, and deeds that

---

104 [Abū Ḥumayd. *Musnad Aḥmad #15477; Al-Ḥizb al-Aʿẓam*]

105 [Abū Hurayrah. *Sunan Ibn Mājah #765*]

106 [Abū Ḥumayd. *Ṣaḥīḥ Muslim #1165*]

107 [Abū Ayyūb al-Anṣārī. *Mustadrak Ḥākim #1540/5942*; Abū Umāmah al-Bāhilī. *Muʿjam al-Kabīr (Ṭabarānī)*]

108 [Um Salamah. *Muʿjam al-Kabīr (Ṭabarānī)*]

مِنْ فَوْقِي نُوْرًا، وَّمِنْ تَحْتِيْ نُوْرًا. اَللّٰهُمَّ أَعْطِنِيْ نُوْرًا۔

﴿١٠٤﴾ اَللّٰهُمَّ افْتَحْ لَنَا أَبْوَابَ رَحْمَتِكَ، وَسَهِّلْ لَنَا أَبْوَابَ رِزْقِكَ۔

﴿١٠٥﴾ اَللّٰهُمَّ اعْصِمْنِيْ مِنَ الشَّيْطَانِ الرَّجِيْمِ۔

﴿١٠٦﴾ اَللّٰهُمَّ إِنِّيْ أَسْأَلُكَ مِنْ فَضْلِكَ۔

﴿١٠٧﴾ اَللّٰهُمَّ اغْفِرْ لِيْ خَطَايَايَ وَذُنُوْبِيْ كُلَّهَا. اَللّٰهُمَّ انْعَشْنِيْ، وَأَحْيِنِيْ، وَارْزُقْنِيْ، وَاهْدِنِيْ لِصَالِحِ الأَعْمَالِ وَالأَخْلَاقِ، إِنَّهُ لَا يَهْدِيْ لِصَالِحِهَا وَلَا يَصْرِفُ سَيِّئَهَا إِلَّا أَنْتَ۔

﴿١٠٨﴾ اَللّٰهُمَّ إِنِّيْ أَسْأَلُكَ رِزْقًا طَيِّبًا، وَّعِلْمًا

will be accepted.

(109) *O Allah, I am Your bondman, son of Your bondman, and son of Your bondwoman. My forelock is in Your Hand. Your command for me prevails. Your Judgment concerning me is justice itself. I beseech You by every name You have, by which You have named Yourself, or which You have revealed in Your Book, or which You taught any one of Your creations, or which You preferred to keep to Yourself in the knowledge of the Unseen with You, to make the Great Qur'ān the life of my heart, the light of my eyes, the remedy of my grief, and the dispeller of my anxiety.*

(110) *O Allah, Lord of Jibrīl (Gabriel), Mīkā'īl (Michael), Isrāfīl, and Lord of Ibrāhīm (Abraham), Ismā'īl (Ishmael), and Is-ḥāq (Isaac), grant me safety and do not impose anyone of Your creations upon me with such a thing as would be intolerable for me.*

---

109 ['Abdullāh ibn Mas'ūd. *Mu'jam al-Kabīr (Ṭabarānī)*]

110 [*Muṣannaf ibn Abī Shaybah* #29171]

نَّافِعًا، وَّعَمَلًا مُّتَقَبَّلًا۔

﴿١٠٩﴾ اَللّٰهُمَّ إِنِّيْ عَبْدُكَ وَابْنُ عَبْدِكَ وَابْنُ أَمَتِكَ، نَاصِيَتِيْ بِيَدِكَ، مَاضٍ فِيَّ حُكْمُكَ، عَدْلٌ فِيَّ قَضَاؤُكَ. أَسْأَلُكَ بِكُلِّ اسْمٍ هُوَ لَكَ، سَمَّيْتَ بِهٖ نَفْسَكَ، أَوْ أَنْزَلْتَهٗ فِيْ كِتَابِكَ، أَوْ عَلَّمْتَهٗ أَحَدًا مِّنْ خَلْقِكَ، أَوِ اسْتَأْثَرْتَ بِهٖ فِيْ عِلْمِ الْغَيْبِ عِنْدَكَ، أَنْ تَجْعَلَ الْقُرْاٰنَ الْعَظِيْمَ رَبِيْعَ قَلْبِيْ، وَنُوْرَ بَصَرِيْ، وَجِلَاءَ حُزْنِيْ، وَذَهَابَ هَمِّيْ۔

﴿١١٠﴾ اَللّٰهُمَّ إِلٰهَ جِبْرِيْلَ وَمِيْكَائِيْلَ وَإِسْرَافِيْلَ، وَإِلٰهَ إِبْرَاهِيْمَ وَإِسْمٰعِيْلَ وَإِسْحٰقَ، عَافِنِيْ وَلَا تُسَلِّطَنَّ أَحَدًا مِّنْ خَلْقِكَ عَلَيَّ بِشَيْءٍ لَّا طَاقَةَ لِيْ بِهٖ۔

(111) *O Allah, protect me from what You declared ḥarām (unlawful) through the sufficiency of what You made halāl (lawful). And make me, by Your benevolence, independent of all besides You.*

(112) *O Allah, You hear my speech and behold my situation. You know my secret and open matters. None of my affairs is concealed from You. And I am the miserable, needy, suppliant, succor-seeking, fearful and anxious person who confesses his sins. I beg of You—the begging of the destitute. I implore You—the imploring of an abased sinner. And I make du'ā' to You—the du'ā' of the fearful afflicted person, whose neck is bowed down before You, whose eyes pour out tears before You, whose body is humbled before You, and whose nose cleaves to the ground for You. O Allah, do not make me frustrated in my supplication to You. And be Compassionate and Merciful to me. O, the Best of those who are asked, and the Best of all who give.*

---

111 ['Alī ibn Abī Ṭālib. *Sunan at-Tirmidhī* #3486]

112 [Composite: 'Abdullāh ibn 'Abbās and 'Abdullāh ibn Ja'far. *Kanz al-'Ummāl* #3614, 3613]

﴿١١١﴾ اَللّٰهُمَّ اكْفِنِيْ بِحَلَالِكَ عَنْ حَرَامِكَ، وَأَغْنِنِيْ بِفَضْلِكَ عَمَّنْ سِوَاكَ۔

﴿١١٢﴾ اَللّٰهُمَّ إِنَّكَ تَسْمَعُ كَلَامِيْ، وَتَرٰى مَكَانِيْ، وَتَعْلَمُ سِرِّيْ وَعَلَانِيَتِيْ، لَا يَخْفٰى عَلَيْكَ شَيْءٌ مِّنْ أَمْرِيْ، وَأَنَا الْبَائِسُ الْفَقِيْرُ، الْمُسْتَغِيْثُ الْمُسْتَجِيْرُ، الْوَجِلُ الْمُشْفِقُ الْمُقِرُّ الْمُعْتَرِفُ بِذَنْبِهٖ۔ أَسْأَلُكَ مَسْأَلَةَ الْمِسْكِيْنِ، وَأَبْتَهِلُ إِلَيْكَ ابْتِهَالَ الْمُذْنِبِ الذَّلِيْلِ، وَأَدْعُوْكَ دُعَاءَ الْخَائِفِ الضَّرِيْرِ، وَدُعَاءَ مَنْ خَضَعَتْ لَكَ رَقَبَتُهٗ، وَفَاضَتْ لَكَ عَبْرَتُهٗ، وَذَلَّ لَكَ جِسْمُهٗ، وَرَغِمَ لَكَ أَنْفُهٗ. اَللّٰهُمَّ لَا تَجْعَلْنِيْ بِدُعَائِكَ شَقِيًّا، وَّكُنْ بِيْ رَءُوْفًا رَّحِيْمًا، يَّا خَيْرَ الْمَسْئُوْلِيْنَ، وَيَا خَيْرَ الْمُعْطِيْنَ۔

O Allah, I place my complaint before You for my weakness, lack of means, and my insignificance in the eyes of people. O the Most Merciful of the merciful, to whom will You entrust me? To an enemy who will oppress me or to the hands of a sympathetic friend whom You have entrusted my affair? (O Allah,) if You are not displeased with me then I do not care for such things. Still, Your protection will be the easier for me.

(113) O Allah, we beg You for yearning hearts that are humble and that turn to Your path.

(114) O Allah, I beg You for faith that settles deep in my heart, a true conviction so that I understand that nothing can afflict me beyond what You have decreed for me, and satisfaction with the provision which You have apportioned for me.

---

113 [ʿAbdullāh ibn Masʿūd. *Mustadrak Ḥākim* #157/1957]

114 [ʿAbdullāh ibn ʿUmar. *Kanz al-ʿUmmāl* #3657; Ibid. *Majmaʿ az-Zawā'id* #17410]

اَللّٰهُمَّ إِلَيْكَ أَشْكُوْ ضُعْفَ قُوَّتِيْ، وَقِلَّةَ حِيْلَتِيْ، وَهَوَانِيْ عَلَى النَّاسِ، يَا أَرْحَمَ الرَّاحِمِيْنَ إِلٰى مَنْ تَكِلُنِيْ؟ إِلٰى عَدُوٍّ يَّتَهَجَّمُنِيْ، أَمْ إِلٰى قَرِيْبٍ مَّلَّكْتَهُ أَمْرِيْ؟ إِنْ لَّمْ تَكُنْ سَاخِطًا عَلَيَّ فَلَا أُبَالِيْ، غَيْرَ أَنَّ عَافِيَتَكَ أَوْسَعُ لِيْ۔

﴿١١٣﴾ اَللّٰهُمَّ إِنَّا نَسْأَلُكَ قُلُوْبًا أَوَّاهَةً مُّخْبِتَةً مُّنِيْبَةً فِيْ سَبِيْلِكَ۔

﴿١١٤﴾ اَللّٰهُمَّ إِنِّيْ أَسْأَلُكَ إِيْمَانًا يُّبَاشِرُ قَلْبِيْ، وَيَقِيْنًا صَادِقًا حَتّٰى أَعْلَمَ أَنَّهُ لَا يُصِيْبُنِيْ إِلَّا مَا كَتَبْتَ لِيْ، وَرِضًى مِّنَ الْمَعِيْشَةِ بِمَا قَسَمْتَ لِيْ۔

(115) O Allah, praise belongs to You just as You say, and better than how we say it.

(116) O Allah, I seek Your protection from bad morals, deeds, desires, and diseases. We seek Your protection from the evil of everything for which Your Prophet Muḥammad ﷺ sought Your protection. And from a bad neighbor where we live, for a bad neighbor in travel moves away. And from domination of the enemy and the ridicule of the enemies. And from hunger; indeed, it is a bad bedfellow. And from betrayal of trust, for it is a bad intimate. And from that we should turn back on our feet, or that we should be persecuted into separation from our religion. And from tribulations both open and hidden, from the bad day, the bad night, the bad moment, and the bad companion.

---

115 [ʿAlī ibn Abī Ṭālib. *Sunan at-Tirmidhī* #3442]

116 [Composite: Quṭbah ibn Mālik. *Kanz al-ʿUmmāl* #3671; Abū Umāmah al-Bāhilī. *Sunan at-Tirmidhī* #3443; Abū Hurayrah. *Mustadrak Ḥākim* #151/1951; ʿAbdullāh ibn ʿAmr ibn al-ʿĀṣ. *Sunan an-Nasāʾī* #5380; Abū Hurayrah. *Sunan an-Nasāʾī* #5373; Ibn Abī Mulaykah. *Ṣaḥīḥ al-Bukhārī* #6104; Zayd ibn Thābit. *Ṣaḥīḥ Muslim* #5112; ʿUqbah ibn ʿĀmir. *Muʿjam al-Kabīr (Ṭabarānī)* 17:294]

﴿١١٥﴾ اَللّٰهُمَّ لَكَ الْحَمْدُ كَالَّذِيْ تَقُوْلُ وَخَيْرًا مِّمَّا نَقُوْلُ.

﴿١١٦﴾ اَللّٰهُمَّ إِنِّيْ أَعُوْذُ بِكَ مِنْ مُّنْكَرَاتِ الْأَخْلَاقِ، وَالْأَعْمَالِ، وَالْأَهْوَاءِ، وَالْأَدْوَاءِ، نَعُوْذُ بِكَ مِنْ شَرِّ مَا اسْتَعَاذَ مِنْهُ نَبِيُّكَ مُحَمَّدٌ صَلَّى اللهُ عَلَيْهِ وَسَلَّمَ، وَمِنْ جَارِ السُّوْءِ فِيْ دَارِ الْمُقَامَةِ فَإِنَّ جَارَ الْبَادِيَةِ يَتَحَوَّلُ، وَغَلَبَةِ الْعَدُوِّ، وَشَمَاتَةِ الْأَعْدَاءِ، وَمِنَ الْجُوْعِ فَإِنَّهُ بِئْسَ الضَّجِيْعُ، وَمِنَ الْخِيَانَةِ فَإِنَّهَا بِئْسَتِ الْبِطَانَةُ، وَأَنْ نَّرْجِعَ عَلٰى أَعْقَابِنَا، أَوْ نُفْتَنَ عَنْ دِيْنِنَا، وَمِنَ الْفِتَنِ مَا ظَهَرَ مِنْهَا وَمَا بَطَنَ، وَمِنْ يَّوْمِ السُّوْءِ، وَمِنْ لَّيْلَةِ السُّوْءِ، وَمِنْ سَاعَةِ السُّوْءِ، وَمِنْ صَاحِبِ السُّوْءِ.

TUESDAY

In the Name of Allah, the Most Compassionate, the Most Merciful

(117) *O Allah, my ṣalāh, my sacrifice, my living, and my dying are all for You. To You is my return and Yours is what I leave behind.*

(118) *O Allah, I beg You for all the good brought by winds.*

(119) *O Allah, make me such that I thank you greatly for Your blessings, I remember You much, I follow Your counsel, and I preserve Your commands. O Allah, our hearts and our limbs are in Your Hand. You did not give us total control over any of them. Since You have done that with these then be their patron, and guide us to the path of rectitude.*

(120) *O Allah, make Your love the dearest and*

117 [ʿAlī ibn Abī Ṭālib. *Sunan at-Tirmidhī* #3442]

118 [ʿAlī ibn Abī Ṭālib. *Kanz al-ʿUmmāl* #3637]

119 [Composite: Abū Hurayrah. *Sunan at-Tirmidhī* #3530; Jābir ibn ʿAbdillāh. *Kanz al-ʿUmmāl* #3644]

120 [Al-Haytham ibn Mālik Aṭ-Ṭāʾī. *Kanz al-ʿUmmāl* #3648]

بِسْمِ اللّٰهِ الرَّحْمٰنِ الرَّحِيْمِ

﴿١١٧﴾ اَللّٰهُمَّ لَكَ صَلَاتِيْ وَنُسُكِيْ وَمَحْيَايَ وَمَمَاتِيْ، وَإِلَيْكَ مَاٰبِيْ، وَلَكَ رَبِّ تُرَاثِيْ۔

﴿١١٨﴾ اَللّٰهُمَّ إِنِّيْ أَسْأَلُكَ مِنْ خَيْرِ مَا تَجِيْءُ بِهِ الرِّيَاحُ۔

﴿١١٩﴾ اَللّٰهُمَّ اجْعَلْنِيْ أُعَظِّمُ شُكْرَكَ، وَأُكْثِرُ ذِكْرَكَ، وَأَتَّبِعُ نَصِيْحَتَكَ، وَأَحْفَظُ وَصِيَّتَكَ۔ اَللّٰهُمَّ إِنَّ قُلُوْبَنَا وَجَوَارِحَنَا بِيَدِكَ، لَمْ تُمَلِّكْنَا مِنْهَا شَيْئًا، فَإِذَا فَعَلْتَ ذٰلِكَ بِهِمَا فَكُنْ أَنْتَ وَلِيَّهُمَا، وَاهْدِنَا إِلٰى سَوَاءِ السَّبِيْلِ۔

﴿١٢٠﴾ اَللّٰهُمَّ اجْعَلْ حُبَّكَ أَحَبَّ الْأَشْيَاءِ إِلَيَّ،

make Your fear the most frightening of all things to me. Cut off worldly needs from me by giving me the longing to meet You. And as You bring comfort to the eyes of the men of the world with their worldly possessions, bring comfort to my eyes with Your obedience and worship.

(121) *O Allah, I beg You for health, chastity, integrity, good character, and acceptance of fate.*

(122) *O Allah, to You is due all praise with thanks; it is only Your domain to do favors with grace. O Allah, I beseech You to enable me to perform the deeds loved by You, develop sincere reliance on You, and hold good expectations from You.*

(123) *O Allah, open my heart to the hearing of Your remembrance.*

---

121 [ʿAbdullāh ibn ʿAmr ibn al-ʿĀṣ. *Kanz al-ʿUmmāl* #3650]

122 [Composite: Kaʿb ibn ʿUjrah and Abū Hurayrah. *Kanz al-ʿUmmāl* #3653, 3654]

123 [ʿAlī ibn Abī Ṭālib. *Kanz al-ʿUmmāl* #3655]

وَاجْعَلْ خَشْيَتَكَ أَخْوَفَ الْأَشْيَاءِ عِنْدِيْ، وَاقْطَعْ عَنِّيْ حَاجَاتِ الدُّنْيَا بِالشَّوْقِ إِلىٰ لِقَائِكَ، وَإِذَا أَقْرَرْتَ أَعْيُنَ أَهْلِ الدُّنْيَا مِنْ دُنْيَاهُمْ فَأَقْرِرْ عَيْنِي مِنْ عِبَادَتِكَ۔

﴿١٢١﴾ اَللّٰهُمَّ إِنِّيْ أَسْأَلُكَ الصِّحَّةَ، وَالْعِفَّةَ، وَالْأَمَانَةَ، وَحُسْنَ الْخُلُقِ، وَالرِّضَا بِالْقَدَرِ۔

﴿١٢٢﴾ اَللّٰهُمَّ لَكَ الْحَمْدُ شُكْرًا وَّلَكَ الْمَنُّ فَضْلًا۔ اَللّٰهُمَّ إِنِّيْ أَسْأَلُكَ التَّوْفِيْقَ لِمَحَابِّكَ مِنَ الْأَعْمَالِ، وَصِدْقَ التَّوَكُّلِ عَلَيْكَ، وَحُسْنَ الظَّنِّ بِكَ۔

﴿١٢٣﴾ اَللّٰهُمَّ افْتَحْ مَسَامِعَ قَلْبِيْ لِذِكْرِكَ،

Grant me obedience to You and to Your Messenger ﷺ and (grant me) performance of deeds according to Your Book.

(124) *O Allah, make me fear You as if I see You all the time until I meet You. Make me blissful as a result of Your taqwā (Your fear and piety); do not make me wretched as a result of Your disobedience.*

(125) *O Allah, extend Your graciousness to me by turning all difficulties into ease, for to make a difficulty easy is very easy for You. And I ask You for ease and forgiveness in the world and in the Hereafter. O Allah, forgive me for indeed You are the Generous Forgiver.*

(126) *O Allah, purify my heart from hypocrisy, my deeds from ostentation and pretension, my tongue from lies, and my eyes from wrongful glances.*

---

124 [Abū Hurayrah. *Majma' az-Zawā'id* #17393]

125 [Composite: Abū Hurayrah and Abū Sa'īd al-Khudrī. *Kanz al-'Ummāl* #3658, 3659]

126 [Um Ma'bad al-Khuzā'iyyah. *Kanz al-'Ummāl* #3660]

وَارْزُقْنِيْ طَاعَتَكَ، وَطَاعَةَ رَسُوْلِكَ، وَعَمَلًا بِكِتَابِكَ۔

﴿١٢٤﴾ اَللّٰهُمَّ اجْعَلْنِيْ أَخْشَاكَ كَأَنِّيْ أَرَاكَ أَبَدًا حَتّٰى أَلْقَاكَ، وَأَسْعِدْنِيْ بِتَقْوَاكَ، وَلَا تُشْقِنِيْ بِمَعْصِيَتِكَ۔

﴿١٢٥﴾ اَللّٰهُمَّ الْطُفْ بِيْ فِيْ تَيْسِيْرِ كُلِّ عَسِيْرٍ، فَإِنَّ تَيْسِيْرَ كُلِّ عَسِيْرٍ عَلَيْكَ يَسِيْرٌ، وَأَسْأَلُكَ الْيُسْرَ وَالْمُعَافَاةَ فِي الدُّنْيَا وَالْاٰخِرَةِ۔ اَللّٰهُمَّ اعْفُ عَنِّيْ فَإِنَّكَ عَفُوٌّ كَرِيْمٌ۔

﴿١٢٦﴾ اَللّٰهُمَّ طَهِّرْ قَلْبِيْ مِنَ النِّفَاقِ، وَعَمَلِيْ مِنَ الرِّيَاءِ، وَلِسَانِيْ مِنَ الْكَذِبِ، وَعَيْنِيْ مِنَ الْخِيَانَةِ،

For, indeed, You know what the eyes deceptively glance at and what the hearts conceal.

(127) *O Allah, grant me profusely weeping eyes that comfort the heart with tears that flow out of Your fear—before the time comes when eyes will be shedding blood and teeth will become embers.*

(128) *O Allah, grant me security with Your power, admit me to Your mercy, let me spend my entire life in Your obedience, let my life end with my best deed, and make Paradise its reward.*

(129) *O Allah, the Soother of worry, the Remover of grief, the Grantor of the du'ā' of the helpless, the Giver of mercy and compassion in the world and the Hereafter, You alone can have true mercy on me. So show such mercy to me that will totally free me from the need of others' mercy.*

---

127 [ʿAbdullāh ibn ʿUmar. *Kanz al-ʿUmmāl* #3661]

128 [ʿAbdullāh ibn ʿUmar. *Kanz al-ʿUmmāl* #3662]

129 [ʿĀ'ishah. *Mustadrak Ḥākim* #98/1898]

فَإِنَّكَ تَعْلَمُ خَائِنَةَ الْأَعْيُنِ وَمَا تُخْفِي الصُّدُوْرُ۔

﴿١٢٧﴾ اَللّٰهُمَّ ارْزُقْنِيْ عَيْنَيْنِ هَطَّالَتَيْنِ، تَشْفِيَانِ الْقَلْبَ بِذُرُوْفِ الدُّمُوْعِ مِنْ خَشْيَتِكَ، قَبْلَ أَنْ تَكُوْنَ الدُّمُوْعُ دَمًا وَّالْأَضْرَاسُ جَمْرًا۔

﴿١٢٨﴾ اَللّٰهُمَّ عَافِنِيْ فِيْ قُدْرَتِكَ، وَأَدْخِلْنِيْ فِيْ رَحْمَتِكَ، وَاقْضِ أَجَلِيْ فِيْ طَاعَتِكَ، وَاخْتِمْ لِيْ بِخَيْرِ عَمَلِيْ، وَاجْعَلْ ثَوَابَهُ الْجَنَّةَ۔

﴿١٢٩﴾ اَللّٰهُمَّ فَارِجَ الْهَمِّ، كَاشِفَ الْغَمِّ، مُجِيْبَ دَعْوَةِ الْمُضْطَرِّيْنَ، رَحْمٰنَ الدُّنْيَا وَالْاٰخِرَةِ وَرَحِيْمَهُمَا، أَنْتَ تَرْحَمُنِيْ فَارْحَمْنِيْ بِرَحْمَةٍ تُغْنِيْنِيْ بِهَا عَنْ رَّحْمَةِ مَنْ سِوَاكَ۔

(130) *O Allah, I beg You for a surprise blessing and seek Your protection from a sudden misfortune.*

(131) *O Allah, Your name is as-Salām (Giver of Peace); peace comes only from You and returns to You. I beg You, O the Majestic and Benevolent, that You accept our du'ā's, grant us what we long for, and free us from needing those of Your creatures who do not need us.*

(132) *O Allah, choose and select for me.*

(133) *O Allah, make me happy with Your Will, and bless me in whatever has been destined for me so that I do not want to hasten what you delayed or to delay what you hastened.*

(134) *O Allah, there is no (real) life except that of the Hereafter.*

---

130 [Anas ibn Mālik. *'Amal al-Yawm wal-Laylah (Ibn as-Sunnī)* #39]

131 [Abū Sa'īd al-Khudrī. *Majma' az-Zawā'id* #16998]

132 [Abū Bakr. *Sunan at-Tirmidhī* #3438]

133 ['Abdullāh ibn 'Umar. *Kanz al-'Ummāl* #9323]

134 [Anas ibn Mālik. *Ṣaḥīḥ al-Bukhārī* #2741]

﴿١٣٠﴾ اَللّٰهُمَّ إِنِّيْ أَسْأَلُكَ مِنْ فُجَاءَةِ الْخَيْرِ، وَأَعُوْذُ بِكَ مِنْ فُجَاءَةِ الشَّرِّ۔

﴿١٣١﴾ اَللّٰهُمَّ أَنْتَ السَّلَامُ وَمِنْكَ السَّلَامُ وَإِلَيْكَ يَعُوْدُ السَّلَامُ، أَسْأَلُكَ يَا ذَا الْجَلَالِ وَالْإِكْرَامِ أَنْ تَسْتَجِيْبَ لَنَا دَعْوَتَنَا، وَأَنْ تُعْطِيَنَا رَغْبَتَنَا، وَأَنْ تُغْنِيَنَا عَمَّنْ أَغْنَيْتَهُ عَنَّا مِنْ خَلْقِكَ۔

﴿١٣٢﴾ اَللّٰهُمَّ خِرْ لِيْ وَاخْتَرْ لِيْ۔

﴿١٣٣﴾ اَللّٰهُمَّ أَرْضِنِيْ بِقَضَائِكَ، وَبَارِكْ لِيْ فِيْمَا قُدِّرَ لِيْ، حَتّٰى لَا أُحِبَّ تَعْجِيْلَ مَا أَخَّرْتَ، وَلَا تَأْخِيْرَ مَا عَجَّلْتَ۔

﴿١٣٤﴾ اَللّٰهُمَّ لَا عَيْشَ إِلَّا عَيْشُ الْاٰخِرَةِ۔

(135) O Allah, give me life of a humble person and death of a humble person, and raise me on the Day of Judgment among humble persons.

(136) O Allah, make me among those who, when they commit an act of virtue, rejoice, and when they commit a mistake, seek forgiveness.

(137) O Allah, I beg You for Your special mercy with which You may guide my heart, arrange my affairs, end my disorder, improve my religion, discharge my debt, protect that part of me that is out of sight, elevate whatever is in sight, brighten my face, purify my deeds, inspire me with what is right for me, return to me what I cherish and love, and protect me from every evil.

(138) O Allah, grant me faith that is never shak-

---

135 [Anas ibn Mālik. *Sunan at-Tirmidhī* #2275]

136 [ʿĀ'ishah. *Sunan Ibn Mājah* #3810]

137 [ʿAbdullāh ibn ʿAbbās. *Sunan at-Tirmidhī* #3341; *Muʿjam al-Kabīr (Ṭabarānī)* 10/284; *Kanz al-ʿUmmāl* #3608, 4988] All the duʿā's listed here from 137 to 143 are part of one comprehensive duʿā' that Prophet Muḥammad ﷺ said at the end of his nightly *Tahajjud* ṣalāh.

138 Ibid.

﴿١٣٥﴾ اَللّٰهُمَّ أَحْيِنِيْ مِسْكِيْنًا، وَّأَمِتْنِيْ مِسْكِيْنًا، وَّاحْشُرْنِيْ فِيْ زُمْرَةِ الْمَسَاكِيْنِ۔

﴿١٣٦﴾ اَللّٰهُمَّ اجْعَلْنِيْ مِنَ الَّذِيْنَ إِذَا أَحْسَنُوْا اسْتَبْشَرُوْا، وَإِذَا أَسَاءُوْا اسْتَغْفَرُوْا۔

﴿١٣٧﴾ اَللّٰهُمَّ إِنِّيْ أَسْأَلُكَ رَحْمَةً مِّنْ عِنْدِكَ تَهْدِيْ بِهَا قَلْبِيْ، وَتَجْمَعُ بِهَا أَمْرِيْ، وَتَلُمُّ بِهَا شَعَثِيْ، وَتُصْلِحُ بِهَا دِيْنِيْ، وَتَقْضِيْ بِهَا دَيْنِيْ، وَتَحْفَظُ بِهَا غَائِبِيْ، وَتَرْفَعُ بِهَا شَاهِدِيْ، وَتُبَيِّضُ بِهَا وَجْهِيْ، وَتُزَكِّيْ بِهَا عَمَلِيْ، وَتُلْهِمُنِيْ بِهَا رَشَدِيْ، وَتَرُدُّ بِهَا أُلْفَتِيْ، وَتَعْصِمُنِيْ بِهَا مِنْ كُلِّ سُوْءٍ۔

﴿١٣٨﴾ اَللّٰهُمَّ أَعْطِنِيْ إِيْمَانًا لَّا يَرْتَدُّ، وَيَقِيْنًا

en, belief so that there is no disbelief thereafter, and mercy by virtue of which I gain the distinction of honor granted by You in this life and the Hereafter.

(139) *O Allah, I beg You for success in what is predetermined, the hospitality reserved for Your martyrs, the life of the blissful, the company of prophets, and Your help against the enemies; verily You hear all duʿā's.*

(140) *O Allah, if there is any blessing that You have promised to any of Your creations or You are going to give it to any of Your servants, but I have been unable to conceive of it, and my efforts have fallen short of it, and my intentions and supplications have not reached it, then I also long for it and beg You for the same in the name of Your mercy, O Cherisher of the worlds.*

---

139 Ibid.

140 Ibid.

لَّيْسَ بَعْدَهُ كُفْرٌ، وَّرَحْمَةً أَنَالُ بِهَا شَرَفَ كَرَامَتِكَ فِي الدُّنْيَا وَالْاٰخِرَةِ۔

﴿١٣٩﴾ اَللّٰهُمَّ إِنِّيْ أَسْأَلُكَ الْفَوْزَ فِي الْقَضَاءِ، وَنُزُلَ الشُّهَدَاءِ، وَعَيْشَ السُّعَدَاءِ، وَمُرَافَقَةَ الْأَنْبِيَاءِ، وَالنَّصْرَ عَلَى الْأَعْدَاءِ، إِنَّكَ سَمِيْعُ الدُّعَاءِ۔

﴿١٤٠﴾ اَللّٰهُمَّ مَا قَصَّرَ عَنْهُ رَأْيِيْ، وَضَعُفَ عَنْهُ عَمَلِيْ، وَلَمْ تَبْلُغْهُ نِيَّتِيْ وَمَسْأَلَتِيْ مِنْ خَيْرٍ وَّعَدْتَّهُ أَحَدًا مِّنْ خَلْقِكَ، أَوْ خَيْرٍ أَنْتَ مُعْطِيْهِ أَحَدًا مِّنْ عِبَادِكَ، فَإِنِّيْ أَرْغَبُ إِلَيْكَ فِيْهِ، وَأَسْأَلُكَ بِرَحْمَتِكَ رَبَّ الْعٰلَمِيْنَ۔

(141) O Allah, I place my needs before You. Although my thoughts are deficient and my actions weak and wanting, I am in need of Your mercy. So, O the One Who decides all affairs and O the One Who heals the hearts, just as You keep the oceans apart from each other, so keep me away from the punishment of Hell and from seeking destruction (in the Hereafter, due to agonies of Hell) and (protect me) from the tribulations of the grave.

(142) O Allah, O the Maker of strong covenants whose every command is right. I beseech You for peace on the Appointed Day and for Paradise on the Day of Eternity along with those who are close to You and will be watching you, are often busy in kneeling and prostrating before You, and who fulfill their covenants. Surely, You are the Merciful, the Most Loving, and indeed, You do what You will.

(143) O Allah, make us the ones who guide aright and are guided aright, who are neither misguided

141 Ibid.

142 Ibid.

143 Ibid.

﴿١٤١﴾ اَللّٰهُمَّ إِنِّيْ أُنْزِلُ بِكَ حَاجَتِيْ، وَإِنْ قَصَّرَ رَأْيِيْ وَضَعُفَ عَمَلِي افْتَقَرْتُ إِلىٰ رَحْمَتِكَ. فَأَسْأَلُكَ يَا قَاضِيَ الْأُمُوْرِ، وَيَا شَافِيَ الصُّدُوْرِ، كَمَا تُجِيْرُ بَيْنَ الْبُحُوْرِ، أَنْ تُجِيْرَنِيْ مِنْ عَذَابِ السَّعِيْرِ، وَمِنْ دَعْوَةِ الثُّبُوْرِ، وَمِنْ فِتْنَةِ الْقُبُوْرِ.

﴿١٤٢﴾ اَللّٰهُمَّ ذَا الْحَبْلِ الشَّدِيْدِ، وَالْأَمْرِ الرَّشِيْدِ، أَسْأَلُكَ الْأَمْنَ يَوْمَ الْوَعِيْدِ، وَالْجَنَّةَ يَوْمَ الْخُلُوْدِ، مَعَ الْمُقَرَّبِيْنَ الشُّهُوْدِ، الرُّكَّعِ السُّجُوْدِ، الْمُوْفِيْنَ بِالْعُهُوْدِ، إِنَّكَ رَحِيْمٌ وَّدُوْدٌ، وَّإِنَّكَ تَفْعَلُ مَا تُرِيْدُ.

﴿١٤٣﴾ اَللّٰهُمَّ اجْعَلْنَا هَادِيْنَ مُهْتَدِيْنَ، غَيْرَ ضَالِّيْنَ وَلَا مُضِلِّيْنَ، سِلْمًا لِّأَوْلِيَائِكَ، وَحَرْبًا

nor do they lead others astray. At peace with Your friends, at war with Your enemies. Loving with Your love those who love You. Despising with Your antagonism those of Your creatures who oppose You. O Allah, this is the supplication and it is up to You to grant it. This is the effort and the reliance is on You.

(144) *O Allah, do not leave me to my own devices even for the twinkling of an eye. Do not take back from me any good that You have granted me.*

(145) *O Allah, You are not a god who might have been devised by us, nor are You a perishable lord invented by us. Nor do You have any partners that share in Your Authority. Nor is it that we had a different god before You whom we would be petitioning rather than You. And it is not that anyone helped You in our creation so we would associate him with You. You are, indeed, Blissful and Supreme.*

---

144 [ʿAbdullāh ibn ʿUmar. *Majmaʿ az-Zawāʾid* #17409]

145 [Ṣuhayb ar-Rūmī. *Kanz al-ʿUmmāl* #3676; Ibid. *Kanz al-ʿUmmāl* #3740.]

لِّأَعْدَائِكَ، نُحِبُّ بِحُبِّكَ مَنْ أَحَبَّكَ، وَنُعَادِيْ بِعَدَاوَتِكَ مَنْ خَالَفَكَ مِنْ خَلْقِكَ۔

اَللّٰهُمَّ هٰذَا الدُّعَاءُ وَعَلَيْكَ الْإِجَابَةُ، وَهٰذَا الْجُهْدُ وَعَلَيْكَ التُّكْلَانُ۔

﴿١٤٤﴾ اَللّٰهُمَّ لَا تَكِلْنِيْ إِلٰى نَفْسِيْ طَرْفَةَ عَيْنٍ، وَّلَا تَنْزِعْ مِنِّيْ صَالِحَ مَا أَعْطَيْتَنِيْ۔

﴿١٤٥﴾ اَللّٰهُمَّ إِنَّكَ لَسْتَ بِإِلٰهٍ إِسْتَحْدَثْنَاهُ، وَلَا بِرَبٍّ يَّبِيْدُ ذِكْرُهُ ابْتَدَعْنَاهُ، وَلَا عَلَيْكَ شُرَكَاءُ يَقْضُوْنَ مَعَكَ، وَلَا كَانَ لَنَا قَبْلَكَ مِنْ إِلٰهٍ نَّلْجَأُ إِلَيْهِ وَنَذَرُكَ، وَلَا أَعَانَكَ عَلٰى خَلْقِنَا أَحَدٌ فَنُشْرِكُهُ فِيْكَ، تَبَارَكْتَ وَتَعَالَيْتَ۔

(146) *O Allah, You are the One Who created my soul and You are the One Who will take it back. Its death and life are in Your control. If You keep it alive then protect it. And if You give it death then grant it forgiveness. O Allah, I beg for ʿāfiyah.*

(147) *O Allah, enrich me with knowledge, grace me with forbearance, honor me with taqwa, and adorn me with peace and security.*

(148) *O Allah, may that period not reach me nor should they (my Companions) reach that period when the knowledgeable will not be followed and the gentle will get no regard. The hearts of the people of that age will be like the aʿājim while their language may be Arabic.*

(149) *O Allah, I seek from you an unbreakable promise. I am just a human being. So whichever believer I may have hurt or rebuked*

146 [ʿAbdullāh ibn ʿUmar. *Ṣaḥīḥ Muslim* #4887]

147 [ʿAbdullāh ibn ʿUmar. *Kanz al-ʿUmmāl* #3663]

148 [Abū Hurayrah. *Kanz al-ʿUmmāl* #3686]

149 [Abū Hurayrah. *Ṣaḥīḥ Muslim* #4707]

﴿١٤٦﴾ اَللَّهُمَّ خلقْتَ نَفْسِيْ وَأَنْتَ تَوَفَّاهَا. لَكَ مَمَاتُهَا وَمَحْيَاهَا. إِنْ أَحْيَيْتَهَا فَاحْفَظْهَا، وَإِنْ أَمَتَّهَا فَاغْفِرْ لَهَا. اَللَّهُمَّ إِنِّيْ أَسْأَلُكَ الْعَافِيَةَ۔

﴿١٤٧﴾ اَللّٰهُمَّ أَغْنِنِيْ بِالْعِلْمِ، وَزَيِّنِّيْ بِالْحِلْمِ، وَأَكْرِمْنِيْ بِالتَّقْوٰى، وَجَمِّلْنِيْ بِالْعَافِيَةِ۔

﴿١٤٨﴾ اَللّٰهُمَّ لَا يُدْرِكْنِيْ زَمَانٌ، وَّلَا يُدْرِكُوْا زَمَانًا، لَّا يُتَّبَعُ فِيْهِ الْعَلِيْمُ، وَلَا يُسْتَحْيٰى فِيْهِ مِنَ الْحَلِيْمِ، قُلُوْبُهُمْ قُلُوْبُ الْأَعَاجِمِ، وَأَلْسِنَتُهُمْ أَلْسِنَةُ الْعَرَبِ۔

﴿١٤٩﴾ اَللّٰهُمَّ إِنِّيْ أَتَّخِذُ عِنْدَكَ عَهْدًا لَّنْ تُخْلِفَنِيْهِ، فَإِنَّمَا أَنَا بَشَرٌ، فَأَيُّمَا مُؤْمِنٍ اٰذَيْتُهُ أَوْ شَتَمْتُهُ أَوْ

or ordered to be lashed or cursed then change my action for him into mercy, purification, and a means of closeness to You on the Day of Judgment.

(150) O Allah, I seek Your protection from vitiligo, obstinacy, hypocrisy, bad morals, and the evil of all that only You are aware of. I seek Allah's protection from the state of the people of the Fire and from the Fire, and whatever words and actions bring one close to these. (I seek your protection) from the evil of everything that is under Your control. I seek Your protection from the evil of this day and of that which will come after it. (I seek your protection) from the evil of my self and the evil of Shayṭān and his polytheism. (I seek your protection) from that we should perpetrate evil against ourselves or bring it upon any Muslim. Or that I should commit a mistake or sin that You will not forgive. And from the constriction on the Day of Judgment.

---

150 [Composite: Anas ibn Mālik. *Sunan Abī Dāwūd* #1329; Abū Hurayrah. *Sunan Abī Dāwūd* #1322; Shaddād ibn 'Aws. *Sunan at-Tirmidhī* #3329; Abū Hurayrah. *Sunan at-Tirmidhī* #3523; 'Ā'ishah. *Sunan Ibn Mājah* #3836; 'Alī ibn Abī Ṭālib. *Sunan Abī Dāwūd* #4393; Abū Mālik al-Ash'arī. *Sunan Abī Dāwūd* #4421; 'Abdullāh ibn 'Amr ibn al-'Āṣ. *Sunan at-Tirmidhī* #3452; Zayd ibn Thābit. *Musnad Aḥmad* #20678; 'Ā'ishah. *Sunan an-Nasā'ī* #1599]

جَلَدْتُّهٗ أَوْ لَعَنْتُهٗ، فَاجْعَلْهَا لَهٗ صَلٰوةً وَّزَكٰوةً وَّقُرْبَةً تُقَرِّبُهٗ بِهَا إِلَيْكَ يَوْمَ الْقِيَامَةِ۔

﴿١٥٠﴾ اَللّٰهُمَّ إِنِّيْ أَعُوْذُ بِكَ مِنَ الْبَرَصِ، وَمِنَ الشِّقَاقِ، وَالنِّفَاقِ، وَسُوْءِ الْأَخْلَاقِ، وَمِنْ شَرِّ مَا تَعْلَمُ. أَعُوْذُ بِاللّٰهِ مِنْ حَالِ أَهْلِ النَّارِ، وَمِنَ النَّارِ وَمَا قَرَّبَ إِلَيْهَا مِنْ قَوْلٍ أَوْ عَمَلٍ، وَّمِنْ شَرِّ مَا أَنْتَ اٰخِذٌۢ بِنَاصِيَتِهٖ. وَأَعُوْذُ بِكَ مِنْ شَرِّ مَا فِيْ هٰذَا الْيَوْمِ وَشَرِّ مَا بَعْدَهٗ، وَمِنْ شَرِّ نَفْسِيْ، وَشَرِّ الشَّيْطَانِ وَشِرْكِهٖ، وَأَنْ نَّقْتَرِفَ عَلٰىٓ أَنْفُسِنَا سُوْءً، أَوْ نَجُرَّهٗ إِلٰى مُسْلِمٍ، أَوْ أَكْتَسِبَ خَطِيْئَةً أَوْ ذَنْبًا لَّا تَغْفِرُهٗ، وَمِنْ ضِيْقِ الْمَقَامِ يَوْمَ الْقِيَامَةِ۔

WEDNESDAY

In the Name of Allah, the Most Compassionate, the Most Merciful

(151) *O Allah, protect my chastity and make my matters easy for me.*

(152) *O Allah, I beseech You for completeness of wuḍū' (ablution) and ṣalāh, and perfection of Your pleasure (with me) and of Your forgiveness (for me).*

(153) *O Allah, grant me my book of accounts in my right hand.*

(154) *O Allah, wrap me in Your mercy and protect me from Your punishment.*

(155) *O Allah, make my feet firm on the Bridge on the day that feet will be shaking.*

---

151 [ʿAlī ibn Abī Ṭālib. *Kanz al-ʿUmmāl* #26690; *Al-Ḥizb al-Aʿẓam*]

152 [Ibid. *Kanz al-ʿUmmāl* #26993]

153 [ʿAlī ibn Abī Ṭālib. *Kanz al-ʿUmmāl* #26692]

154 [ʿAlī ibn Abī Ṭālib. *Kanz al-ʿUmmāl* #26690; *Al-Ḥizb al-Aʿẓam*]

155 [ʿAlī ibn Abī Ṭālib. *Kanz al-ʿUmmāl* #26692]

بِسْمِ اللَّهِ الرَّحْمَٰنِ الرَّحِيمِ

﴿١٥١﴾ اَللّٰهُمَّ حَصِّنْ فَرْجِيْ، وَيَسِّرْ لِيْ أَمْرِيْ۔

﴿١٥٢﴾ اَللّٰهُمَّ إِنِّيْ أَسْأَلُكَ تَمَامَ الْوُضُوْءِ، وَتَمَامَ الصَّلٰوةِ، وَتَمَامَ رِضْوَانِكَ، وَتَمَامَ مَغْفِرَتِكَ۔

﴿١٥٣﴾ اَللّٰهُمَّ أَعْطِنِيْ كِتَابِيْ بِيَمِيْنِيْ۔

﴿١٥٤﴾ اَللّٰهُمَّ غَشِّنِيْ بِرَحْمَتِكَ وَجَنِّبْنِيْ عَذَابَكَ۔

﴿١٥٥﴾ اَللّٰهُمَّ ثَبِّتْ قَدَمَيَّ عَلَى الصِّرَاطِ يَوْمَ تَزِلُّ فِيْهِ الْأَقْدَامُ۔

(156) *Oh Allah, make us successful.*

(157) *O Allah, open our hearts with Your remembrance, complete Your blessings on us through Your Grace, and make us from amongst Your pious servants.*

(158) *O Allah, give me the best of what You give to Your pious servants.*

(159) *O Allah, make me live as a Muslim and die as a Muslim.*

(160) *O Allah, punish the infidels, strike awe in their hearts, create dissension in their ranks, and bring down Your chastisement and punishment upon them. O Allah, punish the infidels—be they from the people of the Book or from the*

---

156 [Muʿāwiyah ibn Abī Sufyān. *ʿAmal al-Yawm wal-Laylah (Ibn as-Sunnī)* #92]

157 [Anas ibn Mālik. *ʿAmal al-Yawm wal-Laylah (Ibn as-Sunnī)* #100]

158 [Saʿd ibn Abī Waqqāṣ. *Mustadrak Ḥākim* #75/748]

159 [Samurah ibn Jundub. *Majmaʿ az-Zawāʾid* #2615]

160 [ʿUmar ibn al-Khaṭṭāb. *Al-Adhkār (Imām Nawawī)* #131; *Al-Ḥizb al-Aʿẓam*]

﴿١٥٦﴾ اَللّٰهُمَّ اجْعَلْنَا مُفْلِحِيْنَ۔

﴿١٥٧﴾ اَللّٰهُمَّ افْتَحْ أَقْفَالَ قُلُوْبِنَا بِذِكْرِكَ، وَأَتْمِمْ عَلَيْنا نِعْمَتَكَ مِنْ فَضْلِكَ، وَاجْعَلْنَا مِنْ عِبَادِكَ الصَّالِحِيْنَ۔

﴿١٥٨﴾ اَللّٰهُمَّ اٰتِنِيْ أَفْضَلَ مَا تُؤْتِيْ عِبَادَكَ الصَّالِحِيْنَ۔

﴿١٥٩﴾ اَللّٰهُمَّ أَحْيِنِيْ مُسْلِمًا وَّأَمِتْنِيْ مُسْلِمًا۔

﴿١٦٠﴾ اَللّٰهُمَّ عَذِّبِ الْكَفَرَةَ، وَأَلْقِ فِيْ قُلُوْبِهِمُ الرُّعْبَ، وَخَالِفْ بَيْنَ كَلِمَتِهِمْ، وَأَنْزِلْ عَلَيْهِمْ رِجْزَكَ وَعَذَابَكَ. اَللّٰهُمَّ عَذِّبِ الْكَفَرَةَ أَهْلَ الْكِتَابِ وَالْمُشْرِكِيْنَ الَّذِيْنَ يَجْحَدُوْنَ اٰيَاتِكَ،

polytheists—who reject Your Signs, refute Your messengers, create roadblocks to Your Path, transgress the limits set by You, and call on other deities with You in worship. There is no god except You. Blessed are You and Exalted way above what these unjust people say.

O Allah, forgive me and the believing men and women, and the Muslim men and women. Set them aright and their mutual relationships, create mutual love in them, put faith and wisdom in their hearts, and make them firm on the religion of Your Messenger. Grant that they be grateful for Your blessings on them, and true to their pledge to You. Help them to victory over Your and their enemy, O True Lord.

(161) *Glorified are You. There is no god besides You. Forgive my sins,*

161 [ʿAbdullāh ibn Masʿūd. *Majmaʿ az-Zawāʾid* #2862]

وَيُكَذِّبُوْنَ رُسُلَكَ، وَيَصُدُّوْنَ عَنْ سَبِيْلِكَ، وَيَتَعَدُّوْنَ حُدُوْدَكَ، وَيَدْعُوْنَ مَعَكَ إِلٰهًا اٰخَرَ. لَا إِلٰهَ إِلَّا أَنْتَ، تَبَارَكْتَ وَتَعَالَيْتَ عَمَّا يَقُوْلُ الظّٰلِمُوْنَ عُلُوًّا كَبِيْرًا.

اَللّٰهُمَّ اغْفِرْ لِيْ وَلِلْمُؤْمِنِيْنَ وَالْمُؤْمِنَاتِ، وَالْمُسْلِمِيْنَ وَالْمُسْلِمَاتِ، وَأَصْلِحْهُمْ، وَأَصْلِحْ ذَاتَ بَيْنِهِمْ، وَأَلِّفْ بَيْنَ قُلُوْبِهِمْ، وَاجْعَلْ فِيْ قُلُوْبِهِمُ الْإِيْمَانَ وَالْحِكْمَةَ، وَثَبِّتْهُمْ عَلٰى مِلَّةِ رَسُوْلِكَ، وَأَوْزِعْهُمْ أَنْ يَّشْكُرُوْا نِعْمَتَكَ الَّتِيْ أَنْعَمْتَ عَلَيْهِمْ وَأَنْ يُّوْفُوْا بِعَهْدِكَ الَّذِيْ عَاهَدْتَّهُمْ عَلَيْهِ، وَانْصُرْهُمْ عَلٰى عَدُوِّكَ وَعَدُوِّهِمْ، إِلٰهَ الْحَقِّ۔

﴿١٦١﴾ سُبْحَانَكَ لَا إِلٰهَ غَيْرُكَ، اغْفِرْ لِيْ ذَنْبِيْ،

and put my deeds in order. Indeed You forgive the sins of whomever You will. And You are Very Forgiving, Most Merciful. O the Forgiver, forgive me. O the Grantor of pardons, accept my repentance. O the Most Compassionate, have mercy on me. O the Effacer of sins, efface my sins. O the Clement, have pity on me. O my Lord, enable me to be grateful for Your blessings on me. Give me energy to excel in Your worship.

O Lord, I beg You for all good and I seek Your protection from all evil. Give me good from beginning to end. Give me longing to meet You without my facing a harmful affliction or a tribulation leading me astray. Protect me from evils. And whomever You protect from evils on that Day, You have really showed mercy to him. That is the supreme achievement.

(162) *O Allah, for You alone is all praise. For You alone is all gratitude.*

162 [Abū Saʿīd al-Khudrī. *Kanz al-ʿUmmāl* #22551]

وَأَصْلِحْ لِيْ عَمَلِيْ، إِنَّكَ تَغْفِرُ الذُّنُوْبَ لِمَنْ تَشَاءُ، وَأَنْتَ الْغَفُوْرُ الرَّحِيْمُ. يَا غَفَّارُ اغْفِرْ لِيْ، يَا تَوَّابُ تُبْ عَلَيَّ، يَا رَحْمٰنُ ارْحَمْنِيْ، يَا عَفُوُّ اعْفُ عَنِّيْ، يَا رَءُوْفُ ارْءُفْ بِيْ، يَا رَبِّ أَوْزِعْنِيْ أَنْ أَشْكُرَ نِعْمَتَكَ الَّتِيْ أَنْعَمْتَ عَلَيَّ وَطَوِّقْنِيْ حُسْنَ عِبَادَتِكَ.

يَا رَبِّ أَسْئَلُكَ مِنَ الْخَيْرِ كُلِّهٖ، وَأَعُوذُ بِكَ مِنَ الشَّرِّ كُلِّهٖ. يَا رَبِّ افْتَحْ لِيْ بِخَيْرٍ، وَّاخْتِمْ لِيْ بِخَيْرٍ، وَاٰتِنِيْ شَوْقًا إِلٰى لِقَائِكَ مِنْ غَيْرِ ضَرَّاءَ مُضِرَّةٍ وَّلَا فِتْنَةٍ مُّضِلَّةٍ، وَّقِنِي السَّيِّئَاتِ، وَمَنْ تَقِ السَّيِّئَاتِ يَوْمَئِذٍ فَقَدْ رَحِمْتَهٗ، وَذٰلِكَ هُوَ الْفَوْزُ الْعَظِيْمُ.

﴿١٦٢﴾ اَللّٰهُمَّ لَكَ الْحَمْدُ كُلُّهٗ، وَلَكَ الشُّكْرُ

Yours alone is the entire dominion. To You alone belongs the entire creation. All good is in Your hands alone. And the disposal of all matters ultimately rests in You alone. I beg You for all good and seek protection in You from all evil.

(163) *In the name of Allah besides Whom there is no god and He is the Most Beneficent, Most Merciful. O Allah, relieve me of all worry and grief. O Allah, with Your praise I do move about and my faults I do confess.*

(164) *O Allah, my God and that of Ibrāhīm (Abraham), Is-ḥāq (Isaac), Yaʿqūb (Jacob), and God of Jibrīl (Gabriel), Mīkā'īl (Michael), and Isrāfīl (Israpheel), I beseech You to accept my duʿā' as I am distressed, to guard me in my faith as I am hemmed in by trying circumstances, to extend Your mercy to me as I am delinquent, and to ward away poverty from me as I am destitute.*

---

163 [Anas ibn Mālik. *Kanz al-ʿUmmāl* #17915 and *Akhbār Iṣbahān (Abū Nuʿaym al-Iṣbahānī)* #1105]

164 [Anas ibn Mālik. *ʿAmal al-Yawm wal-Laylah (Ibn as-Sunnī)* #138]

كُلُّهُ، وَلَكَ الْمُلْكُ كُلُّهُ، وَلَكَ الْخَلْقُ كُلُّهُ، بِيَدِكَ
الْخَيْرُ كُلُّهُ، وَإِلَيْكَ يَرْجِعُ الأَمْرُ كُلُّهُ، أَسْأَلُكَ مِنَ
الْخَيْرِ كُلِّهِ، وَأَعُوْذُ بِكَ مِنَ الشَّرِّ كُلِّهِ۔

﴿١٦٣﴾ بِسْمِ اللهِ الَّذِيْ لَا إِلٰهَ غَيْرُهُ الرَّحْمٰنُ
الرَّحِيْمُ، اَللّٰهُمَّ أَذْهِبْ عَنِّي الْهَمَّ وَالْحُزْنَ۔ اَللّٰهُمَّ
بِحَمْدِكَ انْصَرَفْتُ، وَبِذَنْبِي اعْتَرَفْتُ۔

﴿١٦٤﴾ اَللّٰهُمَّ إِلٰهِي وَإِلٰهَ إِبْرَاهِيْمَ وَإِسْحَاقَ
وَيَعْقُوْبَ، وَإِلٰهَ جِبْرِيْلَ وَمِيْكَائِيْلَ وَإِسْرَافِيْلَ،
أَسْأَلُكَ أَنْ تَسْتَجِيْبَ دَعْوَتِيْ فَإِنِّيْ مُضْطَرٌّ،
وَّتَعْصِمَنِيْ فِيْ دِيْنِيْ فَإِنِّيْ مُبْتَلًى، وَّتَنَالَنِي بِرَحْمَتِكَ
فَإِنِّيْ مُذْنِبٌ، وَّتَنْفِيَ عَنِّي الْفَقْرَ فَإِنِّيْ مُتَمَسْكِنٌ۔

(165) O Allah, I beg of You in the name of the right that the beggars have upon You, for a beggar has a right upon You. That everyone of Your male or female servants from the land or sea whose supplication You have granted and to whose call You have readily responded, include us in their applicable supplications. And include them in our applicable supplications to You. And grant peace to us and to them. Accept our du'ā's and theirs. And ignore our faults and theirs. For we believe in what You revealed, and follow the Messenger. So list us among the witnesses (of truth).

(166) O Allah, grant Muḥammad ﷺ the wasīlah, instill in the hearts of the chosen ones his love, and grant him his position among those of the highest rank and his remembrance among those close to You.

(167) O Allah, grant me Your special guidance,

165 [Abū Sa'īd al-Khudrī. *Kanz al-'Ummāl* #4977]

166 [Abū Umāmah al-Bāhilī. *Kanz al-'Ummāl* #3479]

167 ['Abdullāh ibn 'Abbās. *'Amal al-Yawm wal-Laylah (Ibn as-Sunnī)* #133]

﴿١٦٥﴾ اَللّٰهُمَّ إِنِّيْ أَسْأَلُكَ بِحَقِّ السَّائِلِيْنَ عَلَيْكَ، فَإِنَّ لِلسَّائِلِ عَلَيْكَ حَقًّا، أَيَّمَا عَبْدٍ أَوْ أَمَةٍ مِّنْ أَهْلِ الْبَرِّ وَالْبَحْرِ تَقَبَّلْتَ دَعْوَتَهُمْ وَاسْتَجَبْتَ دُعَاءَهُمْ، أَنْ تُشْرِكَنَا فِيْ صَالِحِ مَا يَدْعُوْنَكَ، وَأَنْ تُشْرِكَهُمْ فِيْ صَالِحِ مَا نَدْعُوْكَ، وَأَنْ تُعَافِيَنَا وَإِيَّاهُمْ، وَأَنْ تَقْبَلَ مِنَّا وَمِنْهُمْ، وَأَنْ تَجَاوَزَ عَنَّا وَعَنْهُمْ، فَإِنَّا اٰمَنَّا بِمَا أَنْزَلْتَ وَاتَّبَعْنَا الرَّسُوْلَ، فَاكْتُبْنَا مَعَ الشَّاهِدِيْنَ۔

﴿١٦٦﴾ اَللّٰهُمَّ أَعْطِ مُحَمَّدَ نِ الْوَسِيْلَةَ، وَاجْعَلْ فِي الْمُصْطَفَيْنَ مَحَبَّتَهٗ، وَفِي الْأَعْلَيْنَ دَرَجَتَهٗ، وَفِي الْمُقَرَّبِيْنَ ذِكْرَهٗ۔

﴿١٦٧﴾ اَللّٰهُمَّ اهْدِنِيْ مِنْ عِنْدِكَ، وَأَفِضْ عَلَيَّ

confer upon me Your grace, bestow amply on me Your mercy, and send down upon me Your blessings.

(168) *O Allah, forgive me, have mercy on me, and accept my repentance; verily You are the Grantor of pardons and the Most Merciful.*

(169) *O Allah, I beseech You for the inspiration of the guided, the deeds of the firm believers, the sincerity of the repenters, the determination of the patient, the effort of the God-fearing, the aspirations of the enthusiasts, the devoutness of the pious, and the cognition of the knowledgeable—so that I fear You. O Allah, I beg You for such fear that will restrain me from Your disobedience so that I may act in obedience to You earning Your pleasure. And so that I may repent sincerely out of Your fear. And so that I may achieve sincerity to You to avoid*

---

168 [ʿAbdullāh ibn ʿUmar. *Musnad Aḥmad* #5100]

169 [ʿAbdullāh ibn ʿAbbās. *Kanz al-ʿUmmāl* #21549; Ibid. *Majmaʿ az-Zawāʾid* #3679]

مِنْ فَضْلِكَ، وَانْشُرْ عَلَيَّ مِنْ رَّحْمَتِكَ، وَأَنْزِلْ عَلَيَّ مِنْ بَرَكَاتِكَ.

﴿١٦٨﴾ اَللّٰهُمَّ اغْفِرْ لِيْ، وَارْحَمْنِيْ، وَتُبْ عَلَيَّ، إِنَّكَ أَنْتَ التَّوَّابُ الرَّحِيْمُ.

﴿١٦٩﴾ اَللّٰهُمَّ إِنِّيْ أَسْأَلُكَ تَوْفِيْقَ أَهْلِ الْهُدٰى، وَأَعْمَالَ أَهْلِ الْيَقِيْنِ، وَمُنَاصَحَةَ أَهْلِ التَّوْبَةِ، وَعَزْمَ أَهْلِ الصَّبْرِ، وَجِدَّ أَهْلِ الْخَشْيَةِ، وَطَلَبَ أَهْلِ الرَّغْبَةِ، وَتَعَبُّدَ أَهْلِ الْوَرَعِ، وَعِرْفَانَ أَهْلِ الْعِلْمِ حَتّٰى أَخَافَكَ. اَللّٰهُمَّ إِنِّيْ أَسْأَلُكَ مَخَافَةً تَحْجُزُنِيْ عَنْ مَّعَاصِيْكَ، حَتّٰى أَعْمَلَ بِطَاعَتِكَ عَمَلًا أَسْتَحِقُّ بِهٖ رِضَاكَ، وَحَتّٰى أُنَاصِحَكَ بِالتَّوْبَةِ خَوْفًا مِّنْكَ، وَحَتّٰى أُخْلِصَ لَكَ النَّصِيْحَةَ

embarrassment before You. And so that I may put my trust totally in You. (And I beg You for having) the best expectations from You, O the Glorified, the Creator of light.

(170) *O Allah, do not cause us to suffer sudden destruction, nor seize us by surprise, nor hasten us (to death) out of rights and wills.*

(171) *O Allah, comfort me in my desolation in the grave. O Allah, have mercy on me by dint of the Great Qur'ān and make it my leader, light, guidance, and mercy. O Allah, make me remember whatever I forget from it. Teach me whatever part of it I do not understand. Endow me with its recitation during the hours of the day and the night. And make it an evidence for me, O Lord of the worlds.*

(172) *O Allah, I am Your bondman, son of Your bondman, and son of Your bondwoman.*

---

170 [ʿAbdullāh ibn Masʿūd. *Majmaʿ az-Zawā'id* #3226]

171 [Composite: Abū Umāmah al-Bāhilī. Kanz al-ʿUmmāl #2784; Abū Manṣūr al-Muẓaffar's *Faḍā'il al-Qur'ān* as reported by Ḥafiẓ ʿIraqī in *Takhrīj Aḥādith al-Iḥyā'*]

172 [*Al-Ḥizb al-Aʿẓam*]

حَيَاءً مِّنْكَ، وَحَتّٰى أَتَوَكَّلَ عَلَيْكَ فِي الْأُمُوْرِ كُلِّهَا، وَحُسْنَ الظَّنِّ بِكَ، سُبْحَانَ خَالِقِ النُّوْرِ۔

﴿١٧٠﴾ اَللّٰهُمَّ لَا تُهْلِكْنَا فُجَاءَةً، وَّلَا تَأْخُذْنَا بَغْتَةً، وَّلَا تُعْجِلْنَا عَنْ حَقٍّ وَّلَا وَصِيَّةٍ۔

﴿١٧١﴾ اَللّٰهُمَّ اٰنِسْ وَحْشَتِيْ فِيْ قَبْرِيْ۔ اَللّٰهُمَّ ارْحَمْنِيْ بِالْقُرْاٰنِ الْعَظِيْمِ، وَاجْعَلْهُ لِيْ إِمَامًا وَّنُوْرًا وَّهُدًى وَّرَحْمَةً. اَللّٰهُمَّ ذَكِّرْنِيْ مِنْهُ مَا نَسِيْتُ، وَعَلِّمْنِيْ مِنْهُ مَا جَهِلْتُ، وَارْزُقْنِيْ تِلَاوَتَهٗ اٰنَاءَ اللَّيْلِ وَأَطْرَافَ النَّهَارِ، وَاجْعَلْهُ لِيْ حُجَّةً يَّا رَبَّ الْعٰلَمِيْنَ۔

﴿١٧٢﴾ اَللّٰهُمَّ أَنَا عَبْدُكَ وَابْنُ عَبْدِكَ وَابْنُ

My forehead is in Your hands. I move around under Your control. I testify to the meeting with You. I believe in Your promise. You commanded me but I disobeyed. You forbade me but I committed. This is the place of the seekers of protection from You against the Fire. There is no god except You. Glorified are You. I have wronged my soul so forgive me. Indeed no one can forgive sins except You.

(173) *O Allah, all praise is for You. Complaints are submitted to You. Cries for help are made to You. Help is sought from You. There is no power or strength except through the help of Allah.*

(174) *O Allah, I seek protection in Your pleasure from Your anger, and in Your forgiveness from Your punishment. I seek protection in You from You. I cannot fully enumerate Your praise. You are as You*

---

173 [ʿAbdullāh ibn Masʿūd. *Firdaws al-Akhbār* (Daylamī) #1812]

174 [Composite: ʿĀ'ishah. *Ṣaḥīḥ Muslim* #751; Um Salamah. *Sunan at-Tirmidhī* #3349; ʿAbdullāh ibn Jaʿfar. *Kanz al-ʿUmmāl* #3613; ʿAbdullāh ibn ʿUmar. *Kanz al-ʿUmmāl* #3678; ʿĀ'ishah bint Qudāmah. *Kanz al-ʿUmmāl* #3649]

أَمَتِكَ، نَاصِيَتِيْ بِيَدِكَ، أَتَقَلَّبُ فِيْ قَبْضَتِكَ، وَأُصَدِّقُ بِلِقَائِكَ، وَأُوْمِنُ بِوَعْدِكَ. أَمَرْتَنِيْ فَعَصَيْتُ، وَنَهَيْتَنِيْ فَأَتَيْتُ، هٰذَا مَقَامُ الْعَائِذِ بِكَ مِنَ النَّارِ، لَا إِلٰهَ إِلَّا أَنْتَ سُبْحَانَكَ، ظَلَمْتُ نَفْسِيْ فَاغْفِرْ لِيْ، إِنَّهٗ لَا يَغْفِرُ الذُّنُوْبَ إِلَّا أَنْتَ۔

﴿١٧٣﴾ اَللّٰهُمَّ لَكَ الْحَمْدُ، وَإِلَيْكَ الْمُشْتَكٰى، وَبِكَ الْمُسْتَغَاثُ، وَأَنْتَ الْمُسْتَعَانُ، وَلَا حَوْلَ وَلَا قُوَّةَ إِلَّا بِاللّٰهِ۔

﴿١٧٤﴾ اَللّٰهُمَّ إِنِّيْ أَعُوْذُ بِرِضَاكَ مِنْ سَخَطِكَ، وَبِمُعَافَاتِكَ مِنْ عُقُوْبَتِكَ، وَأَعُوْذُ بِكَ مِنْكَ، لَا أُحْصِيْ ثَنَاءً عَلَيْكَ، أَنْتَ كَمَا أَثْنَيْتَ عَلٰى نَفْسِكَ۔

have praised Yourself. O Allah, we seek Your protection from erring; from misleading others; from doing injustice to others or receiving injustices from them; from treating others with ignorance or being treated with ignorance; from misleading others or being misled by them. I seek protection in the Light of Your Countenance—which has illuminated the heavens and lighted the darknesses and which sets aright all affairs of this world and the Hereafter—from that You should allow Your anger and bring down Your displeasure on me. Your good will is to be constantly sought until You are pleased. There is no power or strength except through You. O Allah, I seek protection the way You protect a little baby. O Allah, I seek Your protection from the two blind forces: flood and attacking (mad) camel.

اَللّٰهُمَّ إِنَّا نَعُوْذُ بِكَ مِنْ أَنْ نَزِلَّ، أَوْ نُضِلَّ، أَوْ نَظْلِمَ، أَوْ نُظْلَمَ، أَوْ نَجْهَلَ، أَوْ يُجْهَلَ عَلَيْنَا، أَوْ أَضِلَّ، أَوْ أُضَلَّ۔ أَعُوْذُ بِنُوْرِ وَجْهِكَ الْكَرِيْمِ الَّذِيْ أَضَاءَتْ لَهُ السَّمٰوٰتُ، وَأَشْرَقَتْ لَهُ الظُّلُمَاتُ، وَصَلُحَ عَلَيْهِ أَمْرُ الدُّنْيَا وَالْاٰخِرَةِ، أَنْ تُحِلَّ عَلَيَّ غَضَبَكَ، أَوْ تُنْزِلَ عَلَيَّ سَخَطَكَ، وَلَكَ الْعُتْبٰى حَتّٰى تَرْضٰى، وَلَا حَوْلَ وَلَا قُوَّةَ إِلَّا بِكَ۔ اَللّٰهُمَّ وَاقِيَةً كَوَاقِيَةِ الْوَلِيْدِ۔ اَللّٰهُمَّ إِنِّيْ أَعُوْذُ بِكَ مِنْ شَرِّ الْأَعْمَيَيْنِ: السَّيْلِ وَالْبَعِيْرِ الصَّئُوْلِ۔

THURSDAY

In the Name of Allah, the Most Compassionate, the Most Merciful

(175) *O Allah, I beg You in the name of Muḥammad—Your Prophet; Ibrāhīm (Abraham)—Your friend; Mūsā (Moses)—Your confidant; and ʿĪsā (Jesus)—(created by) Your Breath and Your Word; I beg You in the name of the Tawrāt (Torah) of Mūsā, Injīl (Gospel) of Isa, Zabūr (Psalms) of Dāwūd (David), and the Furqān (Criterion, i.e. the Noble Qur'ān) of Muḥammad* ﷺ*—may Allah's blessings and peace be on all of them; I beg You in the name of all the revelations You sent, or judgments You made. (I beg You to grant me) by virtue of every beggar whom You gave, every rich man You made poor, every poor man You made rich, and every misguided person whom You guided; I beg You in that name of Yours that You applied to the earth and it became*

---

175 [Composite: Abū Bakr. *Al-Gharā'ib al-Multaqaṭah min Musnad al-Firdaws* (Ibn Ḥajar) #615; ʿAbdullāh ibn ʿAbbās. *Kanz al-ʿUmmāl* #41326]

بِسْمِ ٱللَّهِ ٱلرَّحْمَٰنِ ٱلرَّحِيمِ

﴿١٧٥﴾ اَللّٰهُمَّ إِنِّيْ أَسْأَلُكَ بِمُحَمَّدٍ نَّبِيِّكَ، وَإِبْرَاهِيْمَ خَلِيْلِكَ، وَمُوسٰى نَجِيِّكَ، وَعِيْسٰى رُوْحِكَ وَكَلِمَتِكَ، وَبِتَوْرَاةِ مُوسٰى، وَإِنْجِيْلِ عِيْسٰى، وَزَبُوْرِ دَاوٗدَ، وَفُرْقَانِ مُحَمَّدٍ صَلَّى اللّٰهُ عَلَيْهِ وَسَلَّمَ وَعَلَيْهِمْ أَجْمَعِيْنَ، وَبِكُلِّ وَحْيٍ أَوْحَيْتَهٗ، أَوْ قَضَاءٍ قَضَيْتَهٗ، أَوْ سَائِلٍ أَعْطَيْتَهٗ، أَوْ غَنِيٍّ أَفْقَرْتَهٗ، أَوْ فَقِيْرٍ أَغْنَيْتَهٗ، أَوْ ضَالٍّ هَدَيْتَهٗ، وَأَسْأَلُكَ بِاسْمِكَ الَّذِيْ وَضَعْتَهٗ عَلَى الْأَرْضِ فَاسْتَقَرَّتْ، وَعَلَى السَّمٰوٰتِ فَاسْتَقَلَّتْ، وَعَلَى الْجِبَالِ فَرَسَتْ، وَأَسْأَلُكَ بِاسْمِكَ الَّذِيْ اسْتَقَرَّ

steady and to the heavens which were thus held up and to the mountains which thus got firmly embedded; and I beg You in that name of Yours by which Your Throne (ʿArsh) was made stationary and in the pure and holy name of Yours which You revealed in Your Book from Your presence; and in that name of Yours which, when You applied to the day it brightened and when You applied to the night it darkened; and in the name of Your greatness, glory, and the light of Your Countenance, (I beg You) that with Your power and strength You endow me with the Great Qur'ān and make it permeate my flesh, blood, ears, and eyes and make my body its practitioner. For indeed there is no power or strength without You. O Allah, do not let us become carefree about Your secret grip, or forget Your remembrance. Do not lift Your cover from us and do not let us become one of the negligent.

(176) *O Allah, I beg You for hastening of good*

---

176 [Composite: ʿĀ'ishah. *Kanz al-ʿUmmāl* #3698; ʿUmar ibn al-Khaṭṭāb and ʿAlī ibn Abī Ṭālib. *Firdaws al-Akhbār* (Daylamī) #1282]

بِهِ عَرْشُكَ، وَأَسْأَلُكَ بِاسْمِكَ الطَّاهِرِ الْمُطَهَّرِ الْمُنَزَّلِ فِيْ كِتَابِكَ مِنْ لَّدُنْكَ، وَبِاسْمِكَ الَّذِيْ وَضَعْتَهٗ عَلَى النَّهَارِ فَاسْتَنَارَ، وَعَلَى اللَّيْلِ فَأَظْلَمَ، وَبِعَظَمَتِكَ وَكِبْرِيَائِكَ، وَبِنُوْرِ وَجْهِكَ أَنْ تَرْزُقَنِيَ الْقُرْاٰنَ الْعَظِيْمَ، وَتُخَلِّطَهٗ بِلَحْمِيْ وَدَمِيْ وَسَمْعِيْ وَبَصَرِيْ، وَتَسْتَعْمِلَ بِهٖ جَسَدِيْ، بِحَوْلِكَ وَقُوَّتِكَ، فَإِنَّهٗ لَا حَوْلَ وَلَا قُوَّةَ إِلَّا بِكَ۔ اَللّٰهُمَّ لَا تُؤْمِنَّا مَكْرَكَ، وَلَا تُنْسِنَا ذِكْرَكَ، وَلَا تَهْتِكْ عَنَّا سِتْرَكَ، وَلَا تَجْعَلْنَا مِنَ الْغَافِلِيْنَ۔

﴿١٧٦﴾ اَللّٰهُمَّ إِنِّيْ أَسْأَلُكَ تَعْجِيْلَ عَافِيَتِكَ،

health from You, patience over my trials sent by You, and exit from this world into Your mercy. O the One Who is sufficient against all and none is sufficient against Him. O the One for the person who has no one. O the Support of the one who has no support. There are no hopes except in You. Liberate me from the state I am in, and help me against what I currently face from that which has befallen me, in the name of Your Gracious Self and by virtue of the right of Muḥammad ﷺ on You. Āmīn.

(177) *O Allah, watch over me with Your Eye that never sleeps, protect me with Your unassailable patronage, and forgive me by virtue of Your power over me so that I may not perish. You are my Hope. How many a bounty there is with which You have favored me; yet little has been my gratitude for that. And how many a trial have You tested me with; yet little has been my patience with that. O the One for Whose bounties my gratitude has been*

---

177 [ʿAlī ibn Abī Ṭālib. *Kanz al-ʿUmmāl* #3441; ʿAlī ibn al-Ḥusayn. *Kanz al-ʿUmmāl* #5014]

وَصَبْرًا عَلىٰ بَلِيَّتِكَ، وَخُرُوْجًا مِّنَ الدُّنْيَا إِلىٰ
رَحْمَتِكَ۔ يَا مَنْ يَّكْفِيْ عَنْ كُلِّ أَحَدٍ، وَّلَا يَكْفِيْ
مِنْهُ أَحَدٌ، يَّا أَحَدَ مَنْ لَّا أَحَدَ لَهٗ، وَيَا سَنَدَ مَنْ
لَّا سَنَدَ لَهُ، انْقَطَعَ الرَّجَاءُ إِلَّا مِنْكَ، نَجِّنِيْ مِمَّا
أَنَا فِيْهِ، وَأَعِنِّيْ عَلىٰ مَا أَنَا عَلَيْهِ مِمَّا نَزَلَ بِيْ، بِجَاهِ
وَجْهِكَ الْكَرِيْمِ، وَبِحَقِّ مُحَمَّدٍ عَلَيْكَ، اٰمِيْنَ۔

﴿١٧٧﴾ اَللّٰهُمَّ احْرُسْنِيْ بِعَيْنِكَ الَّتِيْ لَا تَنَامُ،
وَاكْنُفْنِيْ بِكَنَفِكَ الَّذِيْ لَا يُرَامُ، وَاغْفِرْ لِيْ
بِقُدْرَتِكَ عَلَيَّ فَلَا أَهْلِكُ، وَأَنْتَ رَجَائِيْ. فَكَمْ
مِّنْ نِّعْمَةٍ أَنْعَمْتَ بِهَا عَلَيَّ قَلَّ لَكَ عِنْدَهَا شُكْرِيْ،
وَكَمْ مِّنْ بَلِيَّةٍ اِبْتَلَيْتَنِيْ بِهَا قَلَّ لَكَ عِنْدَهَا صَبْرِيْ.
فَيَا مَنْ قَلَّ عِنْدَ نِعْمَتِهٖ شُكْرِيْ فَلَمْ يَحْرِمْنِيْ، وَيَا

little, yet He did not deprive me. O the One against Whose trial I showed little patience, yet He did not abandon me. O the One Who saw me committing mistakes yet He did not disgrace me.

(178) O the Dispenser of good that will never end, and O the Dispenser of favors that can never be counted, I beseech You to shower blessings on Muḥammad ﷺ and on his family. It is with Your strength alone that I face enemies and oppressors.

(179) O Allah, help me in my religion through my worldly affairs and in my Hereafter through my piety. Look after for me in things that are out of my sight, and do not let me rely upon myself in dealing with those that are before me; O the One Whom sins cannot harm and forgiveness cannot cause any loss, grant me what does not cause you any loss and forgive me what does not harm You. Verily, You are the Generous Giver. O Allah, I beg You

---

178 [ʿAlī ibn Abī Ṭālib. *Kanz al-ʿUmmāl* #3441]

179 [Composite: Jābir ibn ʿAbdillāh. *Kanz al-ʿUmmāl* #5110; ʿAlī ibn Abī Ṭālib. *Firdaws al-Akhbār* (Daylamī) #1913; Ibid. *Kanz al-ʿUmmāl* #5055]

مَنْ قَلَّ عِنْدَ بَلِيَّتِهٖ صَبْرِيْ فَلَمْ يَخْذُلْنِيْ، وَيَا مَنْ رَّاٰنِيْ عَلَى الْخَطَايَا فَلَمْ يَفْضَحْنِيْ۔

﴿١٧٨﴾ يَا ذَا الْمَعْرُوْفِ الَّذِيْ لَا يَنْقَضِيْ أَبَدًا، وَّيَا ذَا النَّعْمَاءِ الَّتِيْ لَا تُحْصٰى أَبَدًا، أَسْأَلُكَ أَنْ تُصَلِّيَ عَلٰى مُحَمَّدٍ، وَعَلٰى اٰلِ مُحَمَّدٍ، وَّبِكَ أَدْرَأُ فِيْ نُحُوْرِ الْأَعْدَاءِ وَالْجَبَّارِيْنَ۔

﴿١٧٩﴾ اَللّٰهُمَّ أَعِنِّيْ عَلٰى دِيْنِيْ بِدُنْيَايَ، وَعَلٰى اٰخِرَتِيْ بِتَقْوَايَ۔ وَاحْفَظْنِيْ فِيْمَا غِبْتُ عَنْهُ، وَلَا تَكِلْنِيْ إِلٰى نَفْسِيْ فِيْمَا حَضَرْتُهٗ، يَا مَنْ لَّا تَضُرُّهُ الذُّنُوْبُ، وَلَا تَنْقُصُهُ الْمَغْفِرَةُ، هَبْ لِيْ مَا لَا يَنْقُصُكَ، وَاغْفِرْ لِيْ مَا لَا يَضُرُّكَ، إِنَّكَ أَنْتَ الْوَهَّابُ. أَسْأَلُكَ فَرَجًا قَرِيْبًا، وَّصَبْرًا جَمِيْلًا،

for quick relief, noble patience, ample sustenance, and safety from all trials; and I beg You for full and lasting protection, gratitude for protection, and independence from other people; there is no turning (away from sin) or strength (to worship) in us except with the help of Allah, Most High and Great.

(180) *O Allah, make my inner self better than my public appearance and make my public appearance righteous. O Allah, I beg You for the good of what You bestow upon people—wealth, family, and children—that they should neither be misled nor misleading.*

(181) *O Allah, make us from among Your chosen servants, with bright faces, arms, and feet, who will be the welcome guests. O Allah, I beg of You a soul satisfied with You—one that believes in meeting with You, is pleased with Your decree, and is content with Your gifts.*

---

180 [ʿUmar ibn al-Khaṭṭāb. *Sunan at-Tirmidhī* #3510]

181 [Composite: Wafd ʿAbd al-Qays. *Musnad Aḥmad* #17163; Abū Umāmah al-Bāhilī. *Muʿjam al-Kabīr (Ṭabarānī)*]

وَرِزْقًا وَاسِعًا، وَالْعَافِيَةَ مِنْ جَمِيعِ الْبَلَاءِ. وَأَسْأَلُكَ تَمَامَ الْعَافِيَةِ، وَأَسْأَلُكَ دَوَامَ الْعَافِيَةِ، وَأَسْأَلُكَ الشُّكْرَ عَلَى الْعَافِيَةِ، وَأَسْأَلُكَ الْغِنٰى عَنِ النَّاسِ، وَلَا حَوْلَ وَلَا قُوَّةَ إِلَّا بِاللهِ الْعَلِيِّ الْعَظِيمِ.

﴿١٨٠﴾ اَللّٰهُمَّ اجْعَلْ سَرِيرَتِي خَيْرًا مِّنْ عَلَانِيَتِي، وَاجْعَلْ عَلَانِيَتِي صَالِحَةً. اَللّٰهُمَّ إِنِّي أَسْأَلُكَ مِنْ صَالِحِ مَا تُؤْتِي النَّاسَ مِنَ الْمَالِ وَالْأَهْلِ وَالْوَلَدِ، غَيْرِ الضَّالِّ وَلَا الْمُضِلِّ.

﴿١٨١﴾ اَللّٰهُمَّ اجْعَلْنَا مِنْ عِبَادِكَ الْمُنْتَخَبِيْنَ، الْغُرِّ الْمُحَجَّلِيْنَ، الْوَفْدِ الْمُتَقَبَّلِيْنَ. اَللّٰهُمَّ إِنِّي أَسْأَلُكَ نَفْسًا بِكَ مُطْمَئِنَّةً تُؤْمِنُ بِلِقَائِكَ، وَتَرْضٰى بِقَضَائِكَ، وَتَقْنَعُ بِعَطَائِكَ.

(182) *O Allah, all praise is due to You, the praise everlasting with Your Eternity. All praise is due to You, the praise which has no end outside Your Will. All praise is due to You, the praise the giver of which seeks but Your pleasure. All praise is due to You, the long lasting praise which is offered with every blink of the eye and with every breath. O Allah, turn my heart to Your religion and protect us from all around with Your mercy. O Allah, make me steadfast, lest I slip, and guide me lest I go astray.*

(183) *O Allah, just as You come between me and my heart, so come between me and the Shayṭān and his machinations. O Allah, endow us with Your bounty, deprive us not of Your sustenance, bless us in what You have bestowed upon us, make our heart free of wants, and put in us the desire for that which is with You.*

---

182 [Composite: ʿAlī ibn Abī Ṭālib. *Kanz al-ʿUmmāl* #3857; Anas ibn Mālik. *Majmaʿ az-Zawā'id* #17383; ʿAbdullāh ibn al-Hād. *Al-Gharā'ib al-Multaqaṭah min Musnad al-Firdaws* (Ibn Ḥajar) #593]

183 [Composite: *Ibid*; ʿAbdullāh ibn ʿAbbās. *Kanz al-ʿUmmāl* #3801]

﴿١٨٢﴾ اَللّٰهُمَّ لَكَ الْحَمْدُ حَمْدًا دَائِمًا مَّعَ خُلُوْدِكَ، وَلَكَ الْحَمْدُ حَمْدًا لَّا مُنْتَهٰى لَهٗ دُوْنَ مَشِيَّتِكَ، وَلَكَ الْحَمْدُ حَمْدًا لَّا يُرِيْدُ قَائِلُهٗ إِلَّا رِضَاكَ، وَلَكَ الْحَمْدُ حَمْدًا مَّلِيًّا عِنْدَ كُلِّ طَرْفَةِ عَيْنٍ وَّتَنَفُّسِ نَفَسٍ۔ اَللّٰهُمَّ أَقْبِلْ بِقَلْبِيْ إِلٰى دِيْنِكَ، وَاحْفَظْ مِنْ وَّرَائِنَا بِرَحْمَتِكَ۔ اَللّٰهُمَّ ثَبِّتْنِيْ أَنْ أَزِلَّ، وَاهْدِنِيْ أَنْ أَضِلَّ۔

﴿١٨٣﴾ اَللّٰهُمَّ كَمَا حُلْتَ بَيْنِيْ وَبَيْنَ قَلْبِيْ فَحُلْ بَيْنِيْ وَبَيْنَ الشَّيْطَانِ وَعَمَلِهٖ۔ اَللّٰهُمَّ ارْزُقْنَا مِنْ فَضْلِكَ، وَلَا تَحْرِمْنَا رِزْقَكَ، وَبَارِكْ لَنَا فِيْمَا رَزَقْتَنَا، وَاجْعَلْ غِنَانَا فِيْ أَنْفُسِنَا، وَاجْعَلْ رَغْبَتَنَا فِيْمَا عِنْدَكَ۔

(184) *O Allah, make me from those who put their trust in You and You became sufficient for them, who sought guidance from You and You guided them, and who sought help from You and You helped them.*

(185) *O Allah, turn the stray thoughts of my heart into Your fear and remembrance. Turn my aspirations and desires toward things of Your liking and pleasure. And when You try me with ease or discomforts, then make me stick to the path of truth and the Sharīʿah of Islam.*

(186) *O Allah, I beg You for the completion of Your blessings in all things and gratitude to You over those until You are pleased and even after Your pleasure. (I beg that) You choose for me in all matters in which there is choice. And make easy choices, not the hard ones for me, O the Generous One.*

---

184 [Anas ibn Mālik. *Kanz al-ʿUmmāl* #5106]

185 [Muhājir ibn Ḥabīb. *Al-Gharā'ib al-Multaqaṭah min Musnad al-Firdaws* (Ibn Ḥajar) #605]

186 [Abū Bakr. *Kanz al-ʿUmmāl* #5034]

﴿١٨٤﴾ اَللّٰهُمَّ اجْعَلْنِيْ مِمَّنْ تَوَكَّلَ عَلَيْكَ فَكَفَيْتَهُ، وَاسْتَهْدَاكَ فَهَدَيْتَهُ، وَاسْتَنْصَرَكَ فَنَصَرْتَهُ۔

﴿١٨٥﴾ اَللّٰهُمَّ اجْعَلْ وَسَاوِسَ قَلْبِيْ خَشْيَتَكَ وَذِكْرَكَ، وَاجْعَلْ هِمَّتِيْ وَهَوَايَ فِيْمَا تُحِبُّ وَتَرْضٰى. اَللّٰهُمَّ وَمَا ابْتَلَيْتَنِيْ بِهٖ مِنْ رَّخَاءٍ وَّشِدَّةٍ فَمَسِّكْنِيْ بِسُنَّةِ الْحَقِّ وَشَرِيْعَةِ الْإِسْلَامِ۔

﴿١٨٦﴾ اَللّٰهُمَّ إِنِّيْ أَسْأَلُكَ تَمَامَ النِّعْمَةِ فِي الْأَشْيَاءِ كُلِّهَا، وَالشُّكْرَ لَكَ عَلَيْهَا حَتّٰى تَرْضٰى وَبَعْدَ الرِّضٰى، وَالْخِيَرَةَ فِيْ جَمِيْعِ مَا يَكُوْنُ فِيْهِ الْخِيَرَةُ، بِجَمِيْعِ مَيْسُوْرِ الْأُمُوْرِ كُلِّهَا، لَا بِمَعْسُوْرِهَا يَا كَرِيْمُ۔

(187) *O Allah, the One Who breaks the dawn and turns the night into an occasion for rest and Who makes the (movement of) the sun and moon a means of keeping time, grant me the strength for jihād in Your way.*

(188) *O Allah, all praise is due to You for the tribulations and actions You direct toward Your creations. All praise is due to You for the tribulations and actions You direct toward our families. All praise is due to You for the tribulations and actions You direct specially toward us. All praise is due to You for guiding us. All praise is due to You for granting us honor. All praise is due to You for covering our faults. All praise is due to You for the Qur'ān. All praise is due to You for our family, property, and grant of safety. Praise is due to You until You are pleased and praise is due to You when You become pleased. O the One Who alone is deserving to be feared. O the One Who alone is capable of forgiving sins.*

---

187 [Abū Saʿīd al-Khudrī. *Firdaws al-Akhbār* (Daylamī) #1989]

188 [Anas ibn Mālik. *Kanz al-ʿUmmāl* #5100]

﴿١٨٧﴾ اَللّٰهُمَّ فَالِقَ الْإِصْبَاحِ وَجَاعِلَ اللَّيْلِ سَكَنًا وَّالشَّمْسِ وَالْقَمَرِ حُسْبَانًا، قَوِّنِيْ عَلَى الْجِهَادِ فِيْ سَبِيْلِكَ۔

﴿١٨٨﴾ اَللّٰهُمَّ لَكَ الْحَمْدُ فِيْ بَلَائِكَ وَصَنِيْعِكَ إِلٰى خَلْقِكَ، وَلَكَ الْحَمْدُ فِيْ بَلَائِكَ وَصَنِيْعِكَ إِلٰى أَهْلِ بُيُوْتِنَا، وَلَكَ الْحَمْدُ فِيْ بَلَائِكَ وَصَنِيْعِكَ إِلٰى أَنْفُسِنَا خَاصَّةً، وَّلَكَ الْحَمْدُ بِمَا هَدَيْتَنَا، وَلَكَ الْحَمْدُ بِمَا أَكْرَمْتَنَا، وَلَكَ الْحَمْدُ بِمَا سَتَرْتَنَا، وَلَكَ الْحَمْدُ بِالْقُرْاٰنِ، وَلَكَ الْحَمْدُ بِالْأَهْلِ وَالْمَالِ، وَلَكَ الْحَمْدُ بِالْمُعَافَاةِ، وَلَكَ الْحَمْدُ حَتّٰى تَرْضٰى، وَلَكَ الْحَمْدُ إِذَا رَضِيْتَ، يَا أَهْلَ التَّقْوٰى، وَيَا أَهْلَ الْمَغْفِرَةِ۔

(189) *O Allah, direct me toward what You like and approve of in my words, actions, deeds, intentions, and courses of action. Indeed You are powerful over all things.*

(190) *O Allah, I seek Your protection from a cunning friend whose eyes are turned to me (with apparent affection) but his heart keeps a watch on me (to find faults); if he sees good, he buries it, and if he sees something bad he announces it. O Allah, I seek Your protection from wretchedness and display of poverty. O Allah, I seek Your protection from the devil and his army. O Allah, I seek Your protection from the sedition of women. O Allah, I seek Your protection from that You should turn Your Face away from me on the Day of Judgment. O Allah, I seek Your protection from actions that*

---

189 [ʿAbdullāh ibn ʿUmar. *Kanz al-ʿUmmāl* #3797]

190 [Composite: Saʿīd al-Maqburī (Mursal). *Kanz al-ʿUmmāl* #3666; Abū Umāmah al-Bāhilī. *ʿAmal al-Yawm wal-Laylah (Ibn as-Sunnī)* #155; Saʿd ibn Abī Waqqāṣ. *Kanz al-ʿUmmāl* #3687; Samurah ibn Jundub. *Majmaʿ az-Zawāʾid* #2615; Anas ibn Mālik. *ʿAmal al-Yawm wal-Laylah (Ibn as-Sunnī)* #120; Abū Hurayrah. *Kanz al-ʿUmmāl* #3775; *Al-Ḥizb al-Aʿẓam*]

﴿١٨٩﴾ اَللّٰهُمَّ وَفِّقْنِي لِمَا تُحِبُّ وَتَرْضٰى مِنَ الْقَوْلِ وَالْعَمَلِ وَالْفِعْلِ وَالنِّيَّةِ وَالْهَدْيِ، إِنَّكَ عَلٰى كُلِّ شَيْءٍ قَدِيْرٌ۔

﴿١٩٠﴾ اَللّٰهُمَّ إِنِّيْ أَعُوْذُ بِكَ مِنْ خَلِيْلٍ مَّاكِرٍ عَيْنَاهُ تَرَيَانِيْ وَقَلْبُهٗ يَرْعَانِيْ، إِنْ رَّاٰى حَسَنَةً دَفَنَهَا وَإِنْ رَّاٰى سَيِّئَةً أَذَاعَهَا۔ اَللّٰهُمَّ إِنِّيْ أَعُوْذُ بِكَ مِنَ الْبُؤْسِ وَالتَّبَاؤُسِ۔ اَللّٰهُمَّ إِنِّيْ أَعُوْذُ بِكَ مِنْ إِبْلِيْسَ وَجُنُوْدِهٖ۔ اَللّٰهُمَّ إِنِّيْ أَعُوْذُ بِكَ مِنْ فِتْنَةِ النِّسَاءِ۔ اَللّٰهُمَّ إِنِّيْ أَعُوْذُ بِكَ مِنْ أَنْ تَصُدَّ عَنِّيْ وَجْهَكَ يَوْمَ الْقِيَامَةِ۔ اَللّٰهُمَّ إِنِّيْ أَعُوْذُ بِكَ مِنْ كُلِّ عَمَلٍ يُّخْزِيْنِيْ، وَأَعُوْذُ بِكَ مِنْ كُلِّ صَاحِبٍ يُّرْدِيْنِيْ، وَأَعُوْذُ بِكَ مِنْ كُلِّ أَمَلٍ يُّلْهِيْنِيْ، وَأَعُوْذُ

would humiliate me, companions who would ruin me, wishes that would distract me, poverty that would make me forget everything, and affluence that would lead me to exorbitance. O Allah, I seek Your protection from a worrisome death and I seek Your protection from a sorrowful death.

بِكَ مِنْ كُلِّ فَقْرٍ يُّنْسِيْنِيْ، وَأَعُوْذُ بِكَ مِنْ كُلِّ غِنًى يُّطْغِيْنِيْ- اَللّٰهُمَّ إِنِّيْ أَعُوْذُ بِكَ مِنْ مَّوْتِ الْهَمِّ، وَأَعُوْذُ بِكَ مِنْ مَّوْتِ الْغَمِّ-

FRIDAY

In the Name of Allah, the Most Compassionate, the Most Merciful

(191) *O Lord, O Lord, O Lord. O Allah, O the Greatest, O the Hearer and Seer of all things, O He Who has no partner or assistant, O the Creator of the sun and the luminous moon, O the Refuge of a fear-stricken destitute, O the Nourisher of the little baby, O the Healer of a fractured bone, I cry unto You like the crying of a poor beggar or that of a helpless blind or emaciated man. I beg of You that You make the Qur'ān the life of my heart and a remedy for my grief.*

(192) *O Lord, give us in this world such and such ___ (here mention your needs); O the Comforter of every lonely person; O the Companion of every person who is alone; O the One Who is near and not remote; O the One Who is present and not*

---

191 [Abū Bakr. *Firdaws al-Akhbār* (Daylamī) #1996]

192 [Composite: Anas ibn Mālik. *Kanz al-'Ummāl* #5103 and *Al-Qawl al-Badī'* (al-Sakhāwī); Ḥudhayfah ibn al-Yamān. *Majma' az-Zawā'id* #17396]

بِسْمِ اللَّهِ الرَّحْمَٰنِ الرَّحِيمِ

﴿١٩١﴾ يَا رَبِّ يَا رَبِّ يَا رَبِّ، اَللّٰهُمَّ يَا كَبِيْرُ يَا سَمِيْعُ يَا بَصِيْرُ، يَا مَنْ لَّا شَرِيْكَ لَهٗ وَلَا وَزِيْرَ لَهٗ، وَيَا خَالِقَ الشَّمْسِ وَالْقَمَرِ الْمُنِيْرِ، وَيَا عِصْمَةَ الْبَائِسِ الْخَائِفِ الْمُسْتَجِيْرِ، وَيَا رَازِقَ الطِّفْلِ الصَّغِيْرِ، وَيَا جَابِرَ الْعَظْمِ الْكَسِيْرِ، أَدْعُوْكَ دُعَاءَ الْبَائِسِ الْفَقِيْرِ كَدُعَاءِ الْمُضْطَرِّ الضَّرِيْرِ. أَسْأَلُكَ أَنْ تَجْعَلَ الْقُرْاٰنَ رَبِيْعَ قَلْبِيْ وَجَلَاءَ حُزْنِيْ۔

﴿١٩٢﴾ رَبَّنَا اٰتِنَا فِي الدُّنْيَا (كَذَا وَكَذَا) يَا مُؤْنِسَ كُلِّ وَحِيْدٍ، وَّيَا صَاحِبَ كُلِّ فَرِيْدٍ، وَّيَا قَرِيْبًا غَيْرَ بَعِيْدٍ، وَّيَا شَاهِدًا غَيْرَ غَائِبٍ، وَّيَا غَالِبًا غَيْرَ

away; O the One Who overcomes all and is not overcome; O the Living, the Eternal, the Majestic, and the Benevolent. O the Light of the heavens and the earth. O the Adornment of the heavens and the earth. O the Mighty Sovereign of the heavens and the earth. O the Sole Support of the heavens and the earth. O the Originator of the heavens and the earth. O the Sustainer of the heavens and the earth. O the Majestic and Benevolent. O the Succorer of those crying for help. O the Last Resort of seekers of protection. O the Reliever of the pain of the people in anguish. O the Soother of the grieved ones. O the Acceptor of the du'ā' of desperate supplicants. O the Remover of all pains. O Lord of all the worlds. O the Most Merciful of the merciful, we humbly place all our needs before You.

(193) *O Allah, indeed You are the Mighty Creator of everything. You are the All-Hearing, All-Knowing. You are the Forgiving, the Merciful. You*

---

193 [Composite: Jābir ibn 'Abdillāh. *Firdaws al-Akhbār* (Daylamī) #1800; Ibid. *Kanz al-'Ummāl* #5111; 'Abdullāh ibn Mas'ūd. *Kanz al-'Ummāl* #5087; Abū Hurayrah. *Al-Jāmi' aṣ-Ṣaghīr* #1459]

مَغْلُوْبٍ، يَّا حَيُّ يَا قَيُّوْمُ، يَا ذَا الْجَلَالِ وَالْإِكْرَامِ۔ يَا نُوْرَ السَّمٰوٰتِ وَالْأَرْضِ، يَا زَيْنَ السَّمٰوٰتِ وَالْأَرْضِ، يَا جَبَّارَ السَّمٰوٰتِ وَالْأَرْضِ، يَا عِمَادَ السَّمٰوٰتِ وَالْأَرْضِ، يَا بَدِيْعَ السَّمٰوٰتِ وَالْأَرْضِ، يَا قَيَّامَ السَّمٰوٰتِ وَالْأَرْضِ، يَا ذَا الْجَلَالِ وَالْإِكْرَامِ، يَا صَرِيْخَ الْمُسْتَصْرِخِيْنَ، وَمُنْتَهَى الْعَائِذِيْنَ، وَالْمُفَرِّجُ عَنِ الْمَكْرُوْبِيْنَ، وَالْمُرَوِّحُ عَنِ الْمَغْمُوْمِيْنَ، وَمُجِيْبَ دُعَاءِ الْمُضْطَرِّيْنَ، وَيَا كَاشِفَ الْكَرْبِ، يَا إِلٰهَ الْعٰلَمِيْنَ، وَيَا أَرْحَمَ الرَّاحِمِيْنَ، مَنْزُوْلٌ بِكَ كُلُّ حَاجَةٍ۔

﴿١٩٣﴾ اَللّٰهُمَّ إِنَّكَ خَلَّاقٌ عَظِيْمٌ، إِنَّكَ سَمِيْعٌ عَلِيْمٌ، إِنَّكَ غَفُوْرٌ رَّحِيْمٌ، إِنَّكَ رَبُّ الْعَرْشِ

are the Lord of the Great Throne. O Allah, You are the Most Gracious, the Most Generous, the Benevolent. Forgive me. Have mercy on me. Protect me. Provide me with sustenance. Conceal my faults. Support me. Uplift and elevate me. Guide me aright. Do not let me go astray. And admit me to Paradise through Your mercy, O the Most Merciful of the merciful. O my Lord, in Your Sight make me dear, in my heart make me humble before You, and in the eyes of other people make me honorable. Protect me from bad manners and morals. O Allah, You asked from us that which we do not control except with Your help. So grant us from it that which will make You be pleased with us.

(194) O Allah, I beseech You for abiding faith, a fearful heart, beneficial knowledge, true belief, and the upright religion. I beg of You safety from all mishaps, full and lasting protection,

194 [ʿAlī ibn Abī Ṭālib. *Kanz al-ʿUmmāl* #5055]

الْعَظِيْمِ. اَللّٰهُمَّ إِنَّكَ الْبَرُّ الْجَوَادُ الْكَرِيْمُ، اغْفِرْ لِيْ، وَارْحَمْنِيْ، وَعَافِنِيْ، وَارْزُقْنِيْ، وَاسْتُرْنِيْ، وَاجْبُرْنِيْ، وَارْفَعْنِيْ، وَاهْدِنِيْ، وَلَا تُضِلَّنِيْ، وَأَدْخِلْنِي الْجَنَّةَ، بِرَحْمَتِكَ يَا أَرْحَمَ الرَّاحِمِيْنَ۔ إِلَيْكَ رَبِّيْ فَحَبِّبْنِيْ، وَفِيْ نَفْسِيْ لَكَ رَبِّيْ فَذَلِّلْنِيْ، وَفِيْ أَعْيُنِ النَّاسِ فَعَظِّمْنِيْ، وَمِنْ سَيِّءِ الْأَخْلَاقِ فَجَنِّبْنِيْ۔ اَللّٰهُمَّ إِنَّكَ سَأَلْتَنَا مِنْ أَنْفُسِنَا مَا لَا نَمْلِكُهُ إِلَّا بِكَ، فَأَعْطِنَا مِنْهَا مَا يُرْضِيْكَ عَنَّا۔

﴿١٩٤﴾ اَللّٰهُمَّ إِنِّيْ أَسْأَلُكَ إِيْمَانًا دَائِمًا، وَّأَسْأَلُكَ قَلْبًا خَاشِعًا، وَّأَسْأَلُكَ عِلْمًا نَّافِعًا، وَّأَسْأَلُكَ يَقِيْنًا صَادِقًا، وَّأَسْأَلُكَ دِيْنًا قَيِّمًا، وَّأَسْأَلُكَ الْعَافِيَةَ مِنْ كُلِّ بَلِيَّةٍ، وَّأَسْأَلُكَ تَمَامَ الْعَافِيَةِ، وَأَسْأَلُكَ دَوَامَ

and gratitude for that protection. I seek from You freedom from dependence on other people.

(195) *O Allah, I beg forgiveness for sins which I have repeated after having repented from them before You. I beg forgiveness for all the promises which I have made to You on my behalf and then did not fulfill. I beg forgiveness for Your gifts from which I drew strength only to use it in your disobedience. I beg forgiveness for all those good actions that I intended for Your sake only but later mixed other motives in them. O Allah, do not humiliate me as You do have full knowledge of me and do not punish me as You do have all power over me.*

(196) *O Allah, Lord of the seven heavens and of the Great Throne ('Arsh), be sufficient for me in all matters of concern in whatever way and place You will.*

---

195 ['Abdullāh ibn 'Umar. *Kanz al-'Ummāl* #5126]

196 [Composite: 'Alī ibn Abī Ṭālib. *Kanz al-'Ummāl* #3433]

الْعَافِيَةِ، وَأَسْأَلُكَ الشُّكْرَ عَلَى الْعَافِيَةِ، وَأَسْأَلُكَ الْغِنٰى عَنِ النَّاسِ۔

﴿١٩٥﴾ اَللّٰهُمَّ إِنِّيْ أَسْتَغْفِرُكَ لِمَا تُبْتُ إِلَيْكَ مِنْهُ ثُمَّ عُدْتُّ فِيْهِ، وَأَسْتَغْفِرُكَ لِمَا أَعْطَيْتُكَ مِنْ نَّفْسِيْ ثُمَّ لَمْ أُوْفِ لَكَ بِهٖ، وَأَسْتَغْفِرُكَ لِلنِّعَمِ الَّتِيْ أَنْعَمْتَ بِهَا عَلَيَّ فَتَقَوَّيْتُ بِهَا عَلٰى مَعَاصِيْكَ، وَأَسْتَغْفِرُكَ لِكُلِّ خَيْرٍ أَرَدْتُّ بِهٖ وَجْهَكَ فَخَالَطَنِيْ فِيْهِ مَا لَيْسَ لَكَ. اَللّٰهُمَّ لَا تُخْزِنِيْ فَإِنَّكَ بِيْ عَالِمٌ، وَّلَا تُعَذِّبْنِيْ فَإِنَّكَ عَلَيَّ قَادِرٌ۔

﴿١٩٦﴾ اَللّٰهُمَّ رَبَّ السَّمٰوٰتِ السَّبْعِ وَرَبَّ الْعَرْشِ الْعَظِيْمِ، اكْفِنِيْ كُلَّ مُهِمٍّ مِّنْ حَيْثُ شِئْتَ وَمِنْ أَيْنَ شِئْتَ۔

(197) *Allah is sufficient for me for my religion. Allah is sufficient for my worldly matters. Allah is sufficient for everything that concerns me. Allah is sufficient to take care of anyone who causes aggression against me. Allah is sufficient for me against anyone who is jealous of me. Allah is sufficient for me against anybody who holds evil intentions against me. Allah is sufficient for me at the time of death. Allah is sufficient for me during the questioning (by angels) in the grave. Allah is sufficient for me when my actions are weighed in the balance on the Day of Judgment. Allah is sufficient for me when I have to pass over the Ṣirāṭ Bridge. Allah is enough for me as there is no god besides Him; on Him have I relied and to Him do I turn.*

(198) *O Allah, I seek from You the reward of the grateful, the reception of the close ones, the company of the prophets, the belief of the truthful, the humbleness of the fearful, and the devotion of the true believers—all my life so that You give me death*

---

197 [Buraydah al-Aslamī. *Kashf al-Khafā'* #1134]

198 [Abū Hurayrah. *Kanz al-'Ummāl* #4945]

﴿١٩٧﴾ حَسْبِيَ اللهُ لِدِيْنِي، حَسْبِيَ اللهُ لِدُنْيَايَ، حَسْبِيَ اللهُ لِمَا أَهَمَّنِيْ، حَسْبِيَ اللهُ لِمَنْ بَغٰى عَلَيَّ، حَسْبِيَ اللهُ لِمَنْ حَسَدَنِيْ، حَسْبِيَ اللهُ لِمَنْ كَادَنِيْ بِسُوْءٍ، حَسْبِيَ اللهُ عِنْدَ الْمَوْتِ، حَسْبِيَ اللهُ عِنْدَ الْمَسْأَلَةِ فِي الْقَبْرِ، حَسْبِيَ اللهُ عِنْدَ الْمِيْزَانِ، حَسْبِيَ اللهُ عِنْدَ الصِّرَاطِ، حَسْبِيَ اللهُ لَا إِلٰهَ إِلَّا هُوَ، عَلَيْهِ تَوَكَّلْتُ وَإِلَيْهِ أُنِيْبُ۔

﴿١٩٨﴾ اَللّٰهُمَّ إِنِّيْ أَسْأَلُكَ ثَوَابَ الشَّاكِرِيْنَ، وَنُزُلَ الْمُقَرَّبِيْنَ، وَمُرَافَقَةَ النَّبِيِّيْنَ، وَيَقِيْنَ الصِّدِّيْقِيْنَ، وَذِلَّةَ الْمُتَّقِيْنَ، وَإِخْبَاتَ الْمُوْقِنِيْنَ، حَتّٰى تَوَفَّانِيْ عَلٰى ذٰلِكَ يَا أَرْحَمَ الرَّاحِمِيْنَ۔

in this state, O the Most Merciful of the merciful.

(199) *O Allah, I beseech You by virtue of the blessings You have abundantly poured on me, the good tests that You have subjected me to, and the favors You have bestowed on me, to admit me in Paradise by Your grace, favor, and mercy.*

(200) *O Allah, I beg of You an everlasting faith, upright guidance, and beneficial knowledge.*

(201) *O Allah, indebt me not to an immoral person whom I may have to pay back in this world and in the Hereafter.*

(202) *O Allah, forgive my sins, grant me magnanimity, purify my income, make me content with Your provisions, and let not my heart turn to anything that You have withheld from me.*

---

199 [ʿAbdullāh ibn Masʿūd. *Kanz al-ʿUmmāl* #3784]

200 [Anas ibn Mālik. *Kanz al-ʿUmmāl* #3789]

201 [Muʿādh ibn Jabal. *Kanz al-ʿUmmāl* #3810]

202 [ʿAlī ibn Abī Ṭālib. *Kanz al-ʿUmmāl* #5061]

﴿١٩٩﴾ اَللّٰهُمَّ إِنِّيْ أَسْأَلُكَ بِنِعْمَتِكَ السَّابِغَةِ عَلَيَّ، وَبَلَائِكَ الْحَسَنِ الَّذِيْ ابْتَلَيْتَنِيْ بِهٖ، وَفَضْلِكَ الَّذِيْ أَفْضَلْتَ عَلَيَّ، أَنْ تُدْخِلَنِيَ الْجَنَّةَ بِمَنِّكَ وَفَضْلِكَ وَرَحْمَتِكَ۔

﴿٢٠٠﴾ اَللّٰهُمَّ إِنِّيْ أَسْأَلُكَ إِيْمَانًا دَائِمًا، وَّهَدْيًا قَيِّمًا، وَّعِلْمًا نَّافِعًا۔

﴿٢٠١﴾ اَللّٰهُمَّ لَا تَجْعَلْ لِّفَاجِرٍ عِنْدِيْ نِعْمَةً أُكَافِيْهِ بِهَا فِي الدُّنْيَا وَالْاٰخِرَةِ۔

﴿٢٠٢﴾ اَللّٰهُمَّ اغْفِرْ لِيْ ذَنْبِيْ، وَوَسِّعْ لِيْ خُلُقِيْ، وَطَيِّبْ لِيْ كَسْبِيْ، وَقَنِّعْنِيْ بِمَا رَزَقْتَنِيْ، وَلَا تُذْهِبْ قَلْبِيْ إِلٰى شَيْءٍ صَرَّفْتَهٗ عَنِّيْ۔

(203) O Allah, I seek Your protection from everything You have created and I make You my shelter against them. Grant me with You confidant status, closeness, and a beautiful retreat. Make me among those who are fearful of standing before You and of Your warnings and who look forward to meeting with You. Make me among those who turn to You in sincere repentance. I beseech You for deeds that will be accepted, knowledge that will lead to success, efforts that will be appreciated, and a trade that will suffer no loss.

(204) O Allah, I beg You for release from the Fire. O Allah, help me in the pangs and agonies of death.

(205) O Allah, forgive me, have mercy on me, and join me with the Highest Companion.

---

203 [Composite: Anas ibn Mālik. *Kanz al-ʿUmmāl* #3850; Abū Hurayrah. *Kanz al-ʿUmmāl* #3855]

204 [Composite: Anas ibn Mālik. *Kanz al-ʿUmmāl* #4966; ʿĀ'ishah. *Kanz al-ʿUmmāl* #3629]

205 [ʿĀ'ishah. *Sunan at-Tirmidhī* #3418]

﴿٢٠٣﴾ اَللّٰهُمَّ إِنِّيْ أَسْتَجِيْرُكَ مِنْ جَمِيْعِ كُلِّ شَيْءٍ خَلَقْتَ وَأَحْتَرِسُ بِكَ مِنْهُنَّ. وَاجْعَلْ لِّيْ عِنْدَكَ وَلِيْجَةً، وَّاجْعَلْ لِّيْ عِنْدَكَ زُلْفٰى وَحُسْنَ مَاٰبٍ، وَّاجْعَلْنِيْ مِمَّنْ يَّخَافُ مَقَامَكَ وَوَعِيْدَكَ، وَيَرْجُوْ لِقَائَكَ، وَاجْعَلْنِيْ مِمَّنْ يَّتُوْبُ إِلَيْكَ تَوْبَةً نَّصُوْحًا، وَّأَسْأَلُكَ عَمَلًا مُّتَقَبَّلًا، وَّعِلْمًا نَّجِيْحًا، وَّسَعْيًا مَّشْكُوْرًا، وَّتِجَارَةً لَّنْ تَبُوْرَ.

﴿٢٠٤﴾ اَللّٰهُمَّ إِنِّيْ أَسْأَلُكَ فِكَاكَ رَقَبَتِيْ مِنَ النَّارِ. اَللّٰهُمَّ أَعِنِّيْ عَلٰى غَمَرَاتِ الْمَوْتِ وَسَكَرَاتِ الْمَوْتِ.

﴿٢٠٥﴾ اَللّٰهُمَّ اغْفِرْ لِيْ وَارْحَمْنِيْ وَأَلْحِقْنِيْ بِالرَّفِيْقِ الْأَعْلٰى.

(206) *O Allah, I seek Your protection from that I should join any partner with You knowingly and I seek Your forgiveness if I have ever done so unknowingly. I seek Your protection that any bond of kinship should pray against me because I cut it off. O Allah, I seek Your protection from the evil of that which crawls on its stomach, and the evil of that which walks on two legs, and the evil of that which walks on four legs. O Allah, I seek Your protection from a wife who will make me old ahead of the old age. I seek Your protection from the child who will bring evil consequences to me. I seek Your protection from the wealth that will turn into punishment for me. O Allah, I seek Your protection from harboring any doubts about the Truth after attaining firm conviction. I seek Your protection against the cursed Shayṭān. I seek Your protection from the harm of the Day of Judgment. O Allah I*

---

206 [Composite: Abū Bakr. *Majmaʿ az-Zawā'id* #17670; Zayd ibn Thābit. *Majmaʿ az-Zawā'id* #17059; ʿAbdullāh ibn ʿAbbās. *Kanz al-ʿUmmāl* #3790; Ibid. *Majmaʿ az-Zawā'id* #17429; Al-Barā'. *Kanz al-ʿUmmāl* #3817 and *Firdaws al-Akhbār* (Daylamī) #1882; ʿAbdullāh ibn ʿAmr ibn al-ʿĀṣ. *Kanz al-ʿUmmāl* #3786]

﴿٢٠٦﴾ اَللّٰهُمَّ إِنِّيْ أَعُوْذُ بِكَ مِنْ أَنْ أُشْرِكَ بِكَ شَيْئًا وَّأَنَا أَعْلَمُهُ، وَأَسْتَغْفِرُكَ لِمَا لَا أَعْلَمُ۔ وَأَعُوْذُ بِكَ أَنْ تَدْعُوَ عَلَيَّ رَحِمٌ قَطَعْتُهَا۔ اَللّٰهُمَّ إِنِّيْ أَعُوْذُ بِكَ مِنْ شَرِّ مَنْ يَّمْشِيْ عَلٰى بَطْنِهٖ، وَمِنْ شَرِّ مَنْ يَّمْشِيْ عَلٰى رِجْلَيْنِ، وَمِنْ شَرِّ مَنْ يَّمْشِيْ عَلٰى أَرْبَعٍ۔ اَللّٰهُمَّ إِنِّيْ أَعُوْذُ بِكَ مِنِ امْرَأَةٍ تُشَيِّبُنِيْ قَبْلَ الْمَشِيْبِ، وَأَعُوْذُ بِكَ مِنْ وَّلَدٍ يَّكُوْنُ عَلَيَّ وَبَالًا، وَّأَعُوْذُ بِكَ مِنْ مَّالٍ يَّكُوْنُ عَلَيَّ عَذَابًا۔ اَللّٰهُمَّ إِنِّيْ أَعُوْذُ بِكَ مِنَ الشَّكِّ فِي الْحَقِّ بَعْدَ الْيَقِيْنِ، وَأَعُوْذُ بِكَ مِنَ الشَّيْطَانِ الرَّجِيْمِ، وَأَعُوْذُ بِكَ مِنْ شَرِّ يَوْمِ الدِّيْنِ۔

seek Your protection from a sudden death, snake bite, beasts, drowning, burning, falling on anything, and from being killed with a fleeing troop.

اَللّٰهُمَّ إِنِّيْ أَعُوْذُ بِكَ مِنْ مَّوْتِ الْفُجَاءَةِ، وَمِنْ لَّدْغِ الْحَيَّةِ، وَمِنَ السَّبُعِ، وَمِنَ الْغَرَقِ، وَمِنَ الْحَرَقِ، وَمِنْ أَنْ أَخِرَّ عَلٰى شَيْءٍ، وَّمِنَ الْقَتْلِ عِنْدَ فِرَارِ الزَّحْفِ۔

Concluding Duʿā'

اَللّٰهُمَّ اغْفِرْ ذُنُوْبَنَا، وَاسْتُرْ عُيُوْبَنَا، وَاشْرَحْ صُدُوْرَنَا، وَاحْفَظْ قُلُوْبَنَا، وَنَوِّرْ قُلُوْبَنَا، وَيَسِّرْ أُمُوْرَنَا، وَحَصِّلْ مُرَادَنَا، وَتَمِّمْ تَقْصِيْرَنَا، اَللّٰهُمَّ نَجِّنَا مِمَّا نَخَافُ، يَا حَفِيَّ الْأَلْطَافِ۔

O Allah, forgive our sins, cover our faults, put our minds at rest, protect and enlighten our hearts, facilitate our tasks, let us achieve our goals, make up for our shortcomings, and protect us from whatever we are afraid of. O the One Who is always on the lookout to extend His Kindness!

[This concluding duʿā' was added by Maulwī Muḥammad Shafīʿ Bijnōrī, a disciple of Mawlānā Ashraf ʿAlī Thānawī and an original publisher of the *Munājāt*. Its source is unknown; it has been retained for its obvious beauty and comprehensiveness.]

The Accepted Whispers: Munājāt-e-Maqbūl

WITH TRANSLITERATION

AND COMMENTARY BY KHALID BAIG

This complete edition contains the duʿā's along with their transliteration, translation, and commentary in English. The commentary explains historic background, meanings, merits, and special significance of the duʿā' in question. It also contains detailed references in Arabic.

Reading the commentary once in the beginning and then from time to time later on will help one derive greater benefit from the daily reading of the duʿā's.

176 PP. 5.5 x 8.5 IN. PAPERBACK

Khalid Baig's writing is indeed inspiring. The Accepted Whispers *is no exception. It is a source of immense solace; an orchard lush with spiritual harmony. This is essential reading for the young and the old.*

— MOULANA EBRAHIM BHAM
COUNCIL OF MUSLIM THEOLOGIANS (JAMIATUL ʿULAMA), SOUTH AFRICA

OPEN MIND PRESS
PO BOX 1338, GARDEN GROVE, CA 92842-1338
openmindpress@albalagh.net
www.openmindpress.com

Slippery Stone: An Inquiry Into Islam's Stance on Music

BY KHALID BAIG

This book demystifies the issue of music in Islam by going to original source books in Arabic, many of them brought to light for the first time in the English language. It traces the attitudes of the Muslim society about music throughout its history and quotes extensively from the deliberations of the Qur'ān and Ḥadīth scholars, Sufi masters, and jurists from all schools of Islāmic Law, both Sunnī and Shīʿah.

384 PP. 6 x 9 IN. PAPERBACK

The best compilation to understand the issue of music in Islam. A must read for Muslims of all ages to clarify this controversial issue.

— IMAM TAHIR ANWAR
ZAYTUNA COLLEGE, USA

This work is sure to become a standard reference in its field for many years to come.

— SHAYKH YASIR QADHI
DEAN OF ACADEMIC AFFAIRS, ALMAGHRIB INSTITUTE, USA

. . . well researched and thorough . . . [Its] exposition of the Sufi perspective in chapter eight pulls the carpet from underneath the feet of those who try to justify the introduction of music culture on the basis of the Sufi practice of samāʿ.

— (LATE) DR. MAHMOOD AHMAD GHAZI
FORMER PRESIDENT, INTERNATIONAL ISLAMIC UNIVERSITY, ISLAMABAD

The author deserves credit for bringing into relief in a highly balanced way the Islamic position on music . . . [He] is to be complimented for having addressed a complex issue so astutely and in the truly Islamic perspective.

— THE MUSLIM WORLD BOOK REVIEW

OPEN MIND PRESS
PO BOX 1338, GARDEN GROVE, CA 92842-1338
openmindpress@albalagh.net
www.openmindpress.com